THE LIFE AND LEGACY OF A TRAVELLING
CANINE COMEDY ACT

MY DOGS, MY LIFE

MIKE SANGER

The Book Guild Ltd

First published in Great Britain in 2022 by
The Book Guild Ltd
9 Priory Business Park
Wistow Road, Kibworth
Leicestershire, LE8 0RX
Freephone: 0800 999 2982
www.bookguild.co.uk
Email: info@bookguild.co.uk
Twitter: @bookguild

Typeset in 11pt Minion Pro

Printed and bound in the UK by TJ Books Limited, Padstow, Cornwall

978 1913913 786

British Library Cataloguing in Publication Data.
A catalogue record for this book is available from the British Library.

For
Prince and Candy

A special thanks to Chris Barltrop for his help, advice and encouragement. Victoria Stilwell and Eugène Chaplin for their supporting endorsements, and Rosie Lowe and the team at The Book Guild. My wife Pascale for her support and mutual love for our dogs. My late grandmother Victoria Sanger Freeman for her original idea, and my late father George James Patrick Freeman ('Old Regnas') for leaving me a legacy to live up to.

Every year, I would go to the circus with my mum and dad. After the show we would meet the artists.

Years later I went to a circus festival in France where I discovered a dog act. It was charming and fun. The audience loved it. After the show I met Mike and Pascale, the dog trainers. Mike told me wonderful circus stories. His travels, performances and his dedication to working with his animals.

His book is a witness to a bygone age and changing times.

His sensitivity, his humanity will touch you.

Eugène Chaplin
Curator to the Charlie Chaplin museum

MY DOGS –
MIKE SANGER

Foreword by Victoria Stilwell from the original
American edition

DOGS ENRICH OUR LIVES IN SO many ways. They are loyal, trustworthy companions that have successfully adapted over thousands of years to live with humans. In return they need people to provide them with a safe, supportive and loving environment. They need us to teach them how to survive in our weird domestic world and most of all they need to have our valued attention and time.

This is a story about one man who fulfils this need for all the dogs in his life. Mike Sanger, from the famous Sanger circus family, performs regularly with his dogs. Circus people traditionally lead notoriously tough and nomadic lives, travelling from city to city and performing to audiences of all nationalities. Shouldn't it seem cruel that dogs would be made to endure the same hardship? Not in this case.

Most dogs' behaviour problems stem from the fact that our domestic dogs lead boring, unstimulating lives. In the past, dogs were bred for a specific purpose, helping their owners in their particular areas of expertise – hunting, tracking, guarding, herding, etc. Since those activities have largely faded away, today's dog owners have had to accommodate the domestic dog with various activities such as agility, fly ball and heel to music. These and many other skill sets have been developed to harness dogs' special abilities and provide outlets for their boundless energy. Even those who would normally question whether it is healthy for dogs to perform in a circus would have to agree that introducing such exciting activities would enrich any dog's life. It is wrong to make some animals perform – indeed, it might even be wrong for some dogs, but for Mike Sanger's dogs it is one big game – a time to have fun and do what all dogs are very good at doing – playing!

Most of Sanger's dogs are from rescue situations, some from appalling conditions. These dogs go from being a human's last thought to becoming the most important living creatures in Mike Sanger's life. His dogs are equal members of his family. His training is positive, constructive, and simple – he interacts with the dogs in an "atmosphere of play". Keeping his dogs "happy and mentally balanced", he proves in this book that you don't have to adopt cruel methods when training dogs and shows that dogs respond far better if they actually want to do something.

In my work as a dog trainer and as host of my own dog training TV programme *It's Me or the Dog*, I've found that most troubled dogs lack the attention, physical and mental stimulation, and all-important play time that Mike Sanger so entertainingly describes giving his dogs in this book. Affection, attention, praise and security is the formula for raising a happy, confident dog. He proves it time and time again.

*

Victoria Stilwell is one of the world's most recognised and respected dog trainers. As host of her TV show *It's Me or the Dog* (currently airing on network TV in the UK and over ten other countries) Ms Stilwell has shared her insight and passion for dog training with an ever-broadening audience. Her best-selling book *It's Me or the Dog – How to Have the Perfect Pet* is published in the US by Hyperion.

MEMORIES

1

I'M HOPELESSLY LOST IN THE STREETS of Gothenburg, Sweden, in mid-October. Even with the sun shining, the cold nip in the air warns of approaching winter. I have to ask directions, so I stop an elderly lady and ask the way – a young person surely won't remember the old building.

She tells me how to get there, then asks, "Did you know there was a public outcry when they tore it down?"

I say I haven't heard about that, thank her and continue on in the direction she indicated. I find the church she mentioned and look across the road at a drab car park. This is where the circus building used to stand. It is Sunday, so few cars are parked there.

I walk across the street and stand in the empty spaces marked out with white lines. The sterile, grey bleakness of the car park stands in sharp contrast to my memories of the vibrant, colourful happenings that had been part of this scene all those years ago. I can't suppress my rising nostalgia, and my mind races back to the first time I stood on this spot.

It was around midnight on what had been a very cold day in February 1963. We had journeyed here from Munich, Germany, and the sea crossing from the mainland peninsula of Denmark across the *Kattegat* had been an adventure in itself: the water was covered with solid pack-ice from shore to shore. Sometimes the ship shuddered and groaned as it hit thicker parts of the ice, sounding to us like we had hit a submerged iceberg.

Then, what a change from the tensions of the journey it had been to arrive at our destination, Gothenburg (*Göteborg* in Swedish) and immerse ourselves in the friendly atmosphere that surrounded the old Lorensbergs Cirkus building. The edifice had been built in 1900, replacing an older 1800s building that had burned down, and was designed especially for circus presentations. It was a delightful round, wooden structure, painted green on the outside. It had straight vertical walls and a conical roof that ran up to a cupola. The entire building was about one hundred feet in circumference – not very big for a circus building, even in those days. However, what it lacked in seating capacity – just 1,000–1,500 people – it gained in intimacy and ambiance. The centrepiece of the interior was a natural earth ring covered in sawdust. The ring was surrounded by boxes for the more affluent patrons; behind them, a tiered gallery ran steeply up to the outer walls. In the gangways between the boxes, pillars rose to support the roof. The orchestra was situated on a platform that bridged a gap in the seating; under this platform was a curtained portal through which the artistes entered the ring. Behind the portal, a wide passage connected the ring to the stables; the passage also joined with a labyrinth of smaller passageways leading to the dressing rooms.

Much later when the circus became less of a draw as frontline entertainment, the building hosted rock concerts; Jimmy Hendrix and The Who played there. The Lorensbergs Cirkus building was finally pulled down in 1969. All that survives are two figurative bronze horseheads that now adorn the local fire station entrance.

Becoming aware again of the car park I stand in, I find a bench, sit down and resume my reminiscences. I can clearly smell the unique odour of the circus – a mixture of the ageing painted wood, the pungent redolence of the horse stables, the sawdust in the ring and the faint but ever-present whiff of greasepaint. These smells all combined to produce the circus's unique, unforgettable odour.

I picture in my mind a typical evening as it was then. In 1963, you could say the building was already in its twilight years, but it was still known for the quality shows put on by Cirkus Schumann. The Schumanns had booked Dad to present his act in its annual tour of the big cities of Scandinavia. It was still able to draw a significant audience of loyal circus lovers. The crowds were always in a festive mood as they queued to buy their tickets for the evening's performance. There was no popcorn-munching or cola-guzzling here – European circus audiences in that era were on a par with the opera- or theatre-going public and came to appreciate a good show, not stuff themselves. From the orchestra came the soft, discordant notes of the players tuning their instruments before the overture – a plucked violin string here, a brassy horn note there. Then the lights dimmed, hushing the audience into silent anticipation of the magic about to unfold.

I think of Dad in the ring on the very spot I sit now, with the orchestra playing his entrance music. Together with our donkey, Barny, and our dogs, Prince and Candy, they always worked to a full house. Dad was very popular here and everywhere else he performed. I recall the audience rocking with laughter at the old man being outdone by a donkey and two cheeky canines. As I sit in this place that awakens such strong, pleasurable feelings within me, I become entirely oblivious to my surroundings as a succession of memories spanning the entire gamut of emotions carries me further and further back in time – right to the beginning.

Uncle George, who was the last member of the family to carry the name Sanger, had called a family meeting in my grandparents' big living wagon. The "family" was also the board of directors, and the family business was the "Lord" George Sanger's Circus. It was England, the year was 1956, and I was nine years old. My younger brother Peter and I were sitting on the floor listening to the adults, who sat round the dining table drinking endless cups of tea, as was customary on such occasions.

The living wagon was a typical showman's type of that period. Custom made somewhere in Yorkshire in the late 1940s, it was about twenty-five feet long and stood quite high off the ground on two axles. Steps led up to a veranda where a Dutch door, with separately hinged top and bottom, provided entry. The frame and sides were made of metal and the entire wagon was painted cream on the outside.

The inside was finished in rich oak panelling, with bay windows all round and a kitchen at one end, a bedroom at the other, and a cosy furnished living room in between. Like many things of yesteryear, it was made to last. For my entire childhood it served as a safe, comforting place for me to be. Whenever the family was about to embark on a long journey to get to the next town, they found it necessary to make an early start. On these evenings, Peter and I stayed overnight in our grandparents' wagon so we could remain in bed as the trip began. I would awake in the very early morning to the sounds of men shouting and engines starting. I could hear the clinking and clanking of the trailer being coupled up to the truck, and felt all the more happy snuggled up between new laundered sheets and thick warm blankets. Once we got on the road and the driver kept to a sedate pace, the motion used to rock me back to sleep.

My thoughts return to the family meeting in progress. Those present were Pat Freeman, our father; Victoria (Sanger) Freeman, my grandmother (and Uncle George's sister), called Vicky by most and "Ma" by us kids; and "Da", my grandfather – Jimmy Freeman, otherwise known as "Pimpo", one of the most respected circus performers England has ever known. As testimony to this, in the year 2000 Jimmy was posthumously awarded a special prize by the *World's Fair* – a respected newspaper devoted to the circus profession – recognising him as the "British Circus Performer of the Century".

The only member of our immediate family who was not present at the meeting was our mother, Muriel. Mother was a "Josser" – circus slang for someone not born into circus life. She kept clear of such gatherings and was probably busy preparing lunch in our living trailer. Her father was the owner of a successful garage business in Birmingham.

Mother had met my father towards the end of the Second World War, while she was in the Women's Royal Navy and he was a captain in the Royal West African Frontier Force. Thinking she was marrying just an army officer, I'm sure Mother hadn't a clue what she was getting herself into. But she found out the truth when my father went home on leave and invited her along to meet his parents. That was the first time she had ever set foot on a circus ground.

But love had already taken hold and she embraced her new life, even to partnering with my father in a riding act that went on to work in some of the main circus productions of the time. Her riding career ended when she took a bad fall in a performance co-produced by circus entrepreneur Billy Smart and bandleader Jack Hylton at London's Earl's Court. Thankfully, it didn't cause any permanent disability.

Dad was born into the family when it was enjoying a time of affluence and stability in running the show. He was given a good education and joined the army cadets at an early age. When war broke out, he was selected as officer material and made captain by age twenty-six. After the war, he could have stayed and made a career of the army, but instead, he rejoined the circus and married Mother. He hadn't learned any circus skills before then, but, guided by Da and other members of the family, he threw himself wholeheartedly into learning bareback riding and animal training. He so excelled at these skills that they eventually became his trademark.

The meeting got under way, and the adults discussed next year's programme. "We still need to find two more acts," Uncle George said between sips of tea. "I suggest we try to get Liliane, the contortionist girl from Belgium, back with us. That will be in keeping with our policy of always having one good continental class act. And, as we know from last year, Liliane got the public talking and will be a good draw." Everyone agreed.

Georgy Freeman was one of my grandfather's seven brothers and was over sixty at that time. He'd been with the show for some years with his performing dog act, which was popular with the public and had become a permanent fixture in the annual programme.

"Now," Uncle George said, "the next thing on the agenda is, what shall we do if Georgy Freeman doesn't come back with his dog act? He's thinking of retiring, but we definitely need a dog act in the programme. What about the act we saw last year, performing in that small circus?"

"You mean that one that was playing in the village, and we saw the afternoon show?" Dad asked. Uncle George nodded.

"No, no," Da interjected. "I seem to remember the dogs looked a bit cowed as they performed. George Freeman's dogs look happy when they work – we should have the same kind of act. Maybe their training was too regimental. I would prefer our animals to be and look happy when they perform. That makes me suspicious of their training methods. We want none of that on our show."

Da's firm rebuttal of Uncle George's recommendation put a note of caution into the proceedings, and although a few more dog acts were mentioned, the group couldn't agree who should take over Georgy Freeman's spot.

Now, although Uncle George was considered to be the boss, to my mind, the real brains of that small group was Ma. She was somebody very special – strong-willed and intelligent. Even then, nearing sixty, she retained a regal beauty that turned heads. I remembered hearing about an incident that had occurred many years before, when Alfred Hitchcock was visiting the show. He had planned to use our circus as a backdrop for his 1930 film, *Murder*. Ma was eighteen at the time and very beautiful. One day, while Mr Hitchcock was watching rehearsals, he found himself sitting next to her in the circus tent and promptly asked her to go out with him. She refused on the grounds that her father, with his Victorian attitude, would kill her if he found out. I later came to realise that Ma's beauty wasn't just skin deep. She was a kind, loving person with a strong character, and, on reflection, I realised that she was very mature, even at a young age, and much ahead of her time. She was never afraid to put new ideas forward concerning the circus and throughout her life, even in her nineties, she somehow always stayed in tune with youth.

Up until this point in the family's discussion, Ma had been uncharacteristically silent. I couldn't have guessed that her next contribution would lay the foundation for a unique act that would span two generations, eventually become my livelihood and determine my way of life from that point on.

She spoke suddenly. "Why don't we start our own dog act?" Her remark caught everyone by surprise, but she was prepared and went on to explain her proposal.

"I visualise a character who will be played by Pat – someone like an old rag and bone man riding on a cart pulled by a donkey. He is transporting boxes. When they get to the middle of the ring, the donkey stops and stubbornly refuses to go any farther. Finally, after some funny gags – I still have to work that out with the donkey – Pat offers him a carrot, which persuades him to move forward. As he does, the cart separates from the donkey harness and tips backwards, with Pat taking a fall. The donkey continues on and makes his exit. The boxes that were on the cart are now lying in disarray. Pat gets up and starts to stack them, but that's when a big dog makes his entrance and pushes the boxes down, frustrating

Pat's efforts. That sets the general theme of the act, in which the dog disrupts everything Pat tries to do. I have an idea where a small dog could also be a part of the act. That's the general idea."

No one spoke for some moments – Ma had caught the family's imagination. Uncle George was the first to break the silence.

"It doesn't really sound like a dog act. I mean, the idea is great, but dog acts are when you have ten poodles in the ring all dressed up dancing around on their hind legs and jumping through hoops and things."

"Well, let's be different," Ma said.

In the end, everybody agreed that her idea was a good one and well worth considering. But nobody at that time realised just how good her idea was, and what great appeal this new act would have from that time on.

*

Peter and I were the sixth generation born into the "Lord" George Sanger's Circus. The title "Lord" was bestowed on my great-great-great-grandfather by himself, as a direct result of an incident concerning Buffalo Bill Cody, who came to Europe with his famous "Wild West Show" in the late 1800s. Buffalo Bill's appearance on the scene put him into direct competition with my family's enterprise, which had already been established as the biggest and most important circus of its time in England. Sanger's Circus troupes performed from one end of the British Isles to the other, entering the towns with grand parades of all the animals and performers. Indeed, "Lord" George Sanger's Circus was the first to introduce performances in three rings at the same time – an innovation later copied by the world-famous Barnum & Bailey's Circus.

As most people know, Buffalo Bill bore the honorific of "Colonel". The competition between him and George Sanger was anything but friendly, and one day, George Sanger was heard to remark, "Be damned; if he can call himself a colonel, then I will call myself a 'Lord'!" From that time forward, that is what he did.

Later, "Lord" George was commanded to Balmoral Castle to put on a performance for Queen Victoria. The Queen was so pleased with the show that she thanked Sanger by granting him an audience with Her Majesty. When he was introduced to the Queen as plain "Mr Sanger", Queen Victoria said, "Lord George, I presume."

Whereupon George Sanger replied, "If it pleases your Majesty." Thus, his title was unofficially condoned by the Queen herself, and was never contested by the authorities.

I later learned, however, that, apparently unknown to Lord George, William F. Cody had long been accorded the title of "Colonel" wherever he went – but he had not gained the title through an actual rank earned in the US Army during his years of service as a civilian scout. In 1872, though still a civilian, he was awarded the Congressional Medal of Honor for his heroic actions as a scout at the Battle of Summit Springs on the Platte River, Nebraska, and he was granted the honorary rank of colonel by the Governor of Nebraska as a reward. Their feud notwithstanding, it is fitting that both showmen – "Lord" George and "Colonel" Cody – were gladly accorded their respective honorifics by their millions of fans on both sides of the Atlantic. However, Lord George might take satisfaction today in knowing that he had the last laugh: while his own "title" was validated by Queen Victoria, even if unofficially, the United States government to this day still refuses to recognise Buffalo Bill Cody's rank as "Colonel"!

For all the fame the "Lord" George Sanger's Circus enjoyed in that early era, it gradually lost its importance with the English circus-going public as more commercial shows managed to move ahead with the times better than we did. By 1956, we'd become a family circus in contrast with the circus empire that Lord George once presided over.

Then, in the 1950s, Lord George's descendant, my uncle George Sanger, made some serious business mistakes that unfortunately put the circus on a precarious financial footing. A notable catastrophe was the start-up of a travelling ice show, which was to feature famous ice skaters. The machinery for freezing the water alone cost a fortune in those days. Then there was the special tent Uncle George had constructed, and finally there were the outrageous salaries that had to be paid to the ice-skating stars and cast. The ice production was a flop and we lost a lot of money.

As a young boy, I only vaguely knew about these events, and I loved Uncle George for the kind, eccentric person he was. I remember him tinkering with mechanical projects, much like an absent-minded professor. The Bubble Machine he invented was one example. It consisted of a round metal plate with a miniature moat or trough built into the outer rim. This moat was filled with bubble-making solution. Every six inches or so round the moat were placed little electric motors that each had a spindle with four wire bubble loops on their ends projecting like little propellers. As each motor revolved, the wire loops dipped into the bubble solution; on the "up" movement they were caught in a blast of air from a blowing machine that was fixed to the middle of the plate, forming bubbles. While it was very crude by today's standards, it worked marvellously and was used to great effect in the next season's programme during the finale, showering bubbles all over the inside of the Big Top as the artists paraded around the ring.

During my childhood, the circus did reasonably good business. We had wonderful winter quarters in Horley, in the county of Surrey. The "Farm", as we called it, was directly on the London-to-Brighton road, next to what is now Gatwick Airport. There were fields for the animals to run free in, a big practice barn and an asphalted courtyard to serve as parking for the living trailers. Attached to this land was an ancient, rambling, dilapidated house that is mentioned in the Domesday Book commissioned by William the Conqueror in 1085. (The house was eventually purchased and renovated by Mandy Miller's sister – Miller being an English child film star.) During the summers, when the show was out on tour, we stayed behind with our grandparents, Ma and Da, so we could receive our schooling at Horley Junior. When the show wintered at the farm, we were reunited with our parents. Those were happy days.

When the family first moved to Horley, we had some difficulties to overcome. The local populace learned that circus people were to take up residence in their town, and they assumed we were Gypsies and vagabonds who had no place in their society. On Ma's first shopping trip to the grocers, she was refused service. All the other shops in town did likewise, and there was a general boycott mounted against us. In response, the family, which was quite affluent, ordered a month's supply of food and other necessities from the prestigious London stores, Harrods and Fortnum & Mason. The townspeople watched, dumbfounded, as the convoy of delivery vans, all with the Royal Coat of Arms resplendently painted on their sides, parked in front of the farm. It didn't take them long to comprehend how much business they were losing from these circus "vagabonds", and they soon changed their minds and welcomed Ma with open arms.

*

Another story that fits into the same category – our acceptance by the society around us – concerned Ma and Dad. It happened not long after I was born. Ma's contribution to our moving from town to town entailed driving a big, six-wheel ex-army truck that pulled two trailers behind it. One of these trailers was fondly dubbed the "Queen Mary" because of its huge size, especially in relation to the narrow English country roads of the time. Used for transporting circus paraphernalia and building materials, it was loaded with tent material, canvas and support poles, etc. – but apparently during the Second World War it had been used to carry dismantled Spitfire aircraft via the highways!

Upon arriving in one particular town where the performance was to be given, the truck developed mechanical problems and stalled in a busy intersection, which caused a backup of traffic. Ma sent the person who was riding with her to get help.

Meantime, it didn't take long for a policeman to arrive at the scene of the breakdown. Unfortunately, he had the same ignorant sentiments towards circus people as the Horley shopkeepers. When he saw "CIRCUS" emblazoned on the side of the truck, he took it as licence to lay into Ma nastily, calling her derogatory names.

Ma was mortified and demanded, "How dare you?"

The policeman just laughed at her. He even thought it within his rights to march Ma off to the police station. Sometime later, Dad arrived. The policeman, thinking he was confronting a load of ignorant riff-raff who could hardly read and write, thought he could demean Ma more by subjecting her to a humiliating interrogation well out of proportion to the situation. The policeman demanded a statement or testimony from Ma. What he didn't know was that Dad had a fine education, and in his capacity as an army officer had served on a court martial tribunal – he was fluent in legal terminology and writing. Dad listened to Ma's story and proceeded to write a very convincing statement indeed, recounting how the constable had obviously abused his power and used foul language towards Ma. When the policeman read it, his jaw dropped in disbelief.

About an hour after Ma had been brought into the station, the entire ruckus, which had probably taken place in the charges room, came to the attention of the chief constable. He read the masterpiece my father had written, called the policeman in and demanded that he apologise to Ma.

Another near run-in with the law happened when the circus was on its way to a town in the London suburbs and was driving up the Mall towards Buckingham Palace. These moves were usually done at a very early hour, and it was Mother's job to drive on ahead in a small car to "mark" the road. This entailed chalking down arrows indicating the direction the rest of the circus needed to travel. It was about five o'clock in the morning when Mother was bending down, chalking away in front of the Palace, when the shadow of a policeman darkened her work.

"Eer, eer, wot's goin' on then," asked the policeman in a Cockney accent.

Mother looked up and, being in a joking mood, she said, "Don't you know then? It's for the invasion, so the enemy knows where to go."

The policeman wasn't at all amused, and if Mother hadn't quickly explained properly and said she was sorry quite a few times, he would have trudged her off to the police station.

Another incident comes to mind. Ma's and Uncle George's father, another George, died a few months before I was born. Ma and Uncle George called him "Papa", but to the rest of the family he was known as Grandpa. According to Ma, he was the kindest man on Earth, but he had also inspired fear in her with his strict Victorian discipline. This led her to do a very strange thing. Among the many artistic disciplines she had mastered in the ring were horseback riding, performing with trained pigeons and dancing in a snake act with a python named Freddy. Attired in a belly dancer's costume, she would sway and twirl to Oriental music while entwining the snake about her body in various positions.

Now, as far as I can gather, Freddy was getting on in years and had far outlived the normal lifespan of his species. One day, during her courtship with my grandfather, Vicky returned late from a secret rendezvous with him and had to rush to prepare her act and Freddy for the show. When she went to get Freddy out, she was horrified to find that he was dead in his compartment, quite possibly having died of old age. Ma was aghast, not only because she'd lost Freddy, but also there was no time to replace herself or the snake in the performance, and she was afraid Grandpa would be very angry. But her act was due to go on and she only had a few seconds to think of something.

She decided that if she could just get through this performance, she could break the news more gently to Papa the following day. So she took the poor deceased Freddy and wrapped his body around hers, went into the ring and began her dance, animating the snake from time to time with her own hands. Nobody noticed that Freddy had passed away, and Ma's daring solution remained a secret for many years!

*

Sometime after the family's meeting in Uncle George's wagon to discuss finding two more acts, Georgy Freeman confirmed that he wouldn't be coming back with his dogs. Ma and Dad then went ahead with plans to form the new act. They already had Barny, a donkey that my grandfather used in one of his clown sketches. Mother and Dad then set off to look for suitable dogs at a well-known street market on "Petticoat Lane" in London, where occasionally animals were for sale. They found a dog that was a cross between a collie and German shepherd to take the big dog's part in the act. He was six months old, and they decided to call him Prince. To complete the ensemble, they were able to find a small dog in an animal shelter a few days later. They called her Tiger. With the combined qualities of Ma as choreographer and Dad as the trainer, they managed to put an act together for the coming season. Because of the short time in which they had to prepare, it wasn't the complete routine that Ma had envisioned, but they knew that that would come.

A lot of thought went into finding a name for the act. Again it was Ma who came up with the appropriate title: "Old Regnas". "Old" because Dad would be playing the part of an old man, and

"Regnas" because that was the name "Sanger" turned backwards.

My observations as a young boy of the condition and treatment of the Sanger Circus animals was that they were accepted as equals by the human members. Any animal acquired for the circus automatically became part of our family. I never observed any trauma associated with animal training. An air of calm was always maintained and I never saw Dad lose his cool. As an example, if one of the dogs was experiencing a problem and couldn't get the hang of a new trick, Dad would try a couple of times, and if no progress was being made, he'd just leave it for another day. Then, with him and the dog having slept on it, they'd start the next day with a fresh attitude. Invariably the problem worked itself out so that, without any stress involved, a breakthrough was made.

Fatherly discipline mixed with kindness was the basic formula. Dad never used food as a reward. Instead, affection was a much more potent incentive. The groundwork for training was to make sure the animal understood that a sharp "no" meant that is not the way to do it, while an exclamation of "good boy" and a caress meant he had done well. This method of training might take a long time and require huge amounts of patience, but in the end, when Tiger and Prince were trained, they remained happy and always enjoyed working.

*

The "Lord" George Sanger's Circus, after supplying generations of our family with prosperity, got into difficulty sometime in 1961. Television was gaining in popularity and this saw a change in the public's taste for entertainment, including the circus. The ensuing financial difficulties were at the root of the coming changes to our lives.

The dog act, on the other hand, was getting better. With new ideas being added to the routine, it was evolving into a huge success with audiences and was talked about by professionals of the circus community as a masterpiece. Mr Edward Graves, respected editor of the *World's Fair*, a weekly trade newspaper for circus professionals, wrote in one of his articles: "I predict that Old Regnas and his comedy dog and donkey act will win the hearts of many, if not all." Later, the European agent for the Ringling, Barnum & Bailey Circus – the late "Trolle" Rhodin of Sweden – was asked by someone compiling a book what his favourite dog act of all time was. He said without hesitation, "Old Regnas."

Unfortunately, the success of the dog act couldn't halt the declining finances of the Sanger show. Also, the act suffered a setback when, tragically, Tiger was run over by a truck. It was one of those unfortunate accidents that happened so quickly that no one had time to react. She was sitting on the steps to my grandparents' living wagon when she must have seen or heard another dog. Out of character, she took off like a bullet. The grounds the circus occupied were enclosed within a fence, but somebody had left the gate open. Tiger shot out the gate and straight across the road, where she was hit by a passing truck. She died instantly. Although it affected me, I was at an age where I was impervious to emotions that would affect me now if one of my own dogs met a similar fate. But the grownups of the family were very upset, especially Mother and Ma.

I've heard stories to the contrary, but my own observations have been that when one of my own dog family has died, the other dogs haven't grieved over the one who is gone. As far as I can remember, if Prince grieved for Tiger, he didn't show it but continued to work normally with Barny and Dad.

A short time later, to replace Tiger, Dad found a female dog named Candy in a shelter. She was a mixture of so many different breeds, it is difficult to describe her appearance. She stood about twelve inches high and had a medium long, greyish-brown coat. Her intelligent eyes portrayed a sharp, alert character, which gave promise of her becoming a good working dog. Shortly after finding

Candy, it became evident that she was expecting puppies, so her training was put on hold. When the puppies were born, we found homes for all of them except the one Ma kept as a pet. We had a tradition that when an animal was born on the show, it was named after the town in which he or she was born. So Ma called the puppy "Frome" after the Somerset town the Sanger show was visiting at the time. Frome was Ma's loyal companion for many years.

While Dad was training Candy, he continued working the act with just Barny and Prince. This shortened the act, but because he was working in our own circus, that didn't matter.

To help you understand what was happening during this period to the Sanger show, I should explain that some years previously, Uncle George had found a sponsor to help cover the financial deficit caused by the ice show fiasco. His name was Sharp, and he was the proprietor of a confectionery brand called "Sharp's Toffees". Mr Sharp used to visit the show sometimes but had no direct say in the running of things – he was essentially a silent partner. However, as business continued to get worse, Uncle George had a meeting with Mr Sharp to ask for a further financial commitment. Mr Sharp agreed, but only on the conditions that a manager representing him would travel with the circus full time and all decisions concerning the running of the show had to be discussed with him. I'm sure Uncle George felt he had to agree to those terms, but it was a disastrous move.

The manager, or "Major", as he liked everybody to call him, was an old school friend of Mr Sharp's and came to us straight after leaving the army. He hadn't the slightest idea how to run the business end of the show, so he tried to run things like an army camp, which made the situation absolutely ridiculous. It would have been laughable if you could discount the fact that we were on the verge of losing our way of life to a complete stranger.

As a young boy then, with a rather happy-go-lucky attitude, I didn't realise the stress the grownups of the family must have endured during that time. I wasn't privy to the affairs concerning the running of the circus as they were, but even so, I knew things were seriously wrong when our beloved farm in Horley was sold to pay the accumulating debts. That changed Peter's and my life drastically and put an end to our schooling in Horley, because we had to start travelling with the show. From then on, it wasn't easy for the family to keep up our standard of education while travelling with the circus; we had to visit a different school every three to four days.

During the last few years of his life, my grandfather, Da (Jimmy "Pimpo" Freeman) was bedridden with illness. One winter, the circus was in the Waverley Market, a big exhibition hall on Princes Street in Edinburgh, Scotland, to put on performances during the Christmas holiday. Mother, Peter and I had been packed off to Mother's parents' home in Birmingham to stay for a while. We got word of Da's death while we were away and sadly weren't able to be with him during his last days.

The next winter we went to Billy Smart's Circus in London with the dog act to do a TV appearance. As it happened, it was one of the first TV broadcasts for Eurovision. The act was shown in Germany, where the directors of the foremost German circus saw it, and two weeks afterwards, an offer came for the act to work in Munich at Cirkus Krone. The timing couldn't have been better, because our own circus couldn't last much longer.

I remember that the late fifties through to 1961 were terribly hard – especially the winters. The once-proud "Lord" George Sanger's Circus had been brought down to wintering wherever it could find some inexpensive space to hold our small community of people. That included, in addition to the family performers, one or two steadfast and hardy grooms, the "tent-men" (general workers who help put the tents up), our animals and our wagons. One of the loyal tent-men who'd been around ever since I could remember was Mick. He was a likeable Irishman with a brogue as thick as they come. Uncle George had a soft spot for him, because he liked Mick's quaint live-and-let-live outlook on life. Mick was often drunk, but he always did his work. Rumour had it that sometimes in order to have some of his pay left over for a drink, instead of buying proper food, he bought "Kitty Kat" cat food in tins, because it was cheap. He spread it on bread and swore that it tasted delicious.

The heavy work of building up and pulling down a Big Top circus tent, as well as tending the stables and similar physical tasks, required no qualifications other than brawn. Also, not many questions were asked about the men's backgrounds, so it was no surprise that many drifters and down-and-outs, even criminals, were mixed up with the good men that were hired. There were many stories of the tent-men from the Lord George era, when hundreds of workers had been employed. Some of them, after being laid off in the winter months, would commit a small crime calculated to get them a few months in jail. They would be freed just in time for the circus season to start again.

This brings me to a topic that bugs "real" circus people, because if one of the tent-men was caught in some wrongdoing, "circus people" were blamed. A comparable situation would be if someone working as an unskilled labourer in an automobile factory commits a criminal offence, and it was then said that "the Ford people have committed a crime". To my mind it is an ignorant, lazy and oversimplified way of looking at things, and over the years, this attitude has harmed the reputations of many honest circus performers and the profession as a whole.

But back to our own situation. The relationship with the Major came to a head one day when he said, in his arrogant way, "There should be only one captain of a ship, and in the future, I will be the one to make the decisions here."

It was the last straw for the family. I don't know even to this day how things could have deteriorated to such an extreme, in such a short time, for the family to have lost control of our circus. Some of the staff, sensing a changing tide in the war for control, began to turn their allegiance towards the Major. In particular, one group of artists, smelling the possibility of becoming co-circus proprietors, helped the Major in his efforts to get rid of us. Even one of the tent-men tried to gain favour by reporting to the Major each morning with a salute and calling him "sir".

The last day – or night, as was the case – came after some terrible row with the Major. I was fifteen years old when our family moved off the circus ground, leaving behind the only way of life Ma and Uncle George had ever known. Mr Sharp tried to stop Dad from keeping the dog act, but thank goodness, it wasn't mentioned in the company's bookkeeping records as being part of the Sanger circus assets – so he could do nothing about it. Mother and Dad didn't have much money, but they did have the Cirkus Krone contract and also managed to get an engagement with Billy Smart's Winter Circus in Leeds, England, which would fit in just before they had to leave for Munich. Also, as a direct result of seeing the act on Eurovision, Schumann, the foremost circus of Denmark, wanted the act for the upcoming 1963 summer season.

*

The journey to Munich was one of the worst experiences of my life. With our sparse budget, Dad bought a light van just big enough to transport Barny, Prince, Candy, Mother, Peter, myself, him and the props for the act. We were all crammed in the van with nothing separating us from the dogs and Barny. It was January 1963, and Europe was experiencing one of the most severe winters on record. The channel crossing by ferry to Ostend in Belgium was very rough, and I spent the entire six hours in the boat's restroom throwing up – it was gruesome. When we disembarked and cleared customs, Dad promptly drove up the wrong side of the road and we nearly hit a tram.

We had only three days to complete the journey to Munich, so we had to keep going, with no time to stop and rest in hotels. Dad did all the driving, and thankfully, after some practice, he stayed on the right side of the road. He had to stop now and again to get some sleep, feed the animals and give the dogs a run. I think everybody was suffering, but my big problem was a terrible cramp in my legs. And every time we were forced from exhaustion to stop and rest – we couldn't afford to keep the engine idling while we slept, so the heater was off – it wasn't long before the intense, biting cold woke us up and we wanted to get moving again so we could warm up. Because there were so many of us in the small, confined space, the roof dripped with condensation from our breath, adding dampness to our misery.

To cap that horrible journey, on the last leg not far from Munich, we stopped in a lay-by at the side of the autobahn to give the dogs a run. Peter and I took the opportunity to relieve ourselves. As I peered into the darkness, I could see the faint outline of a litter bin fixed to a tree. Tied up to it and sitting in the bin was a small dog. I let out a cry, which brought Dad on the run. At first I thought the dog was still alive, but at that sub-zero temperature it would have been impossible for any living creature to survive in the open, even for a short time. On closer investigation we could see the glazed look of its unseeing eyes. *How despicable and inhumane*, I thought bitterly, realising how much the dog must have suffered at being abandoned to die in the cold by itself.

We continued our journey, but with the sight of the poor little dog fresh in our minds, we were in a sombre mood when we arrived at the outskirts of Munich. We drove downtown to the Krone Circus building and saw that the evening performance was still in progress. Someone directed us around the back of the building to the warm stables.

A stall had already been prepared for Barny near the other animals. We made sure he had plenty of bedding straw and enough hay to eat. Dad gave Candy and Prince a run and something to eat, but because we had no living trailer with us, the dogs were put into a horse box near Barny, with blankets laid down for them. The stable master assured us the animals would be perfectly safe with their night watchman patrolling and keeping an eye on things. Mother and Dad were ushered into an office by a circus official, where they were given some cash to cover immediate expenses; then we were directed to a very nice hotel. A hot bath and a good night's sleep in a warm bed between crisp, clean sheets was sheer luxury after five nights on the road.

I didn't realise it at the time, but we had left a way of life behind us in England and were entering what was to be a very different lifestyle.

Right from the beginning of rehearsals, Dad's act with Barny and our dogs was a huge success, not only because it was completely different from other, more traditional dog acts, but also because of the way Prince and Candy worked, without any visible commands from Dad. We took the high standard of the act for granted, but the other circus performers were in awe of Dad as a trainer.

The Krone Circus put on three different programmes in their winter building. The first started at Christmas and went through to the end of January, the next ran in February and the final one played in March before the circus started its summer tour through all the major German cities. Our act was only booked for the February programme, but it was so liked by the Munich audiences that Carl Sembach, the boss of Krone, asked Dad to stay on for the March programme. Apparently it was unprecedented for the same act to perform in two separate winter programmes. We couldn't stay for the whole month, because we had to get to Scandinavia to start with Cirkus Schumann, but we stayed for as long as we could, then left for Gothenburg, Sweden, on the fifteenth of March.

The journey was much easier this time. The weather was much better and we were able to stop in hotels along the way. We made our way to the north of Germany, then drove almost all the way to the top of Denmark, where we took a ferry across to Gothenburg, Sweden – and to the old Lorensbergs Cirkus building located downtown.

The Swedish audiences were less lively than the Germans. They hardly ever clapped during a performance, preferring to show their appreciation after the acts were finished and the artists were taking a bow. At first, this was a bit disconcerting for Dad, who'd grown used to the Munich audiences' wild clapping and foot-stomping when he worked. In Germany, even the start of the act got them going, as he made his entrance to his chosen theme, the tune "Colonel Bogey" from the movie *Bridge Over the River Kwai*. The movie had just opened in German cinemas and was very popular. There was Dad, in his old man's costume and makeup, riding in on the cart pulled by Barny to the tune of "Colonel Bogey". It caught the audience's imagination and drove them wild!

So initially, Dad was a little disturbed; he feared that maybe the act wasn't doing so well in Sweden. However, the Schumann family, like many Scandinavians, spoke perfect English, and they reassured Dad the act was well liked and he had nothing to worry about.

After a month in Gothenburg, the circus moved to Stockholm for a month. This time it wasn't to be in a building, but in a Big Top circus tent. The ground was covered with snow and ice, which had to be cleared before they could build the tent up. The managers cast about for a way to clear the grounds. Finally, a drastic but ingenious solution was found, and the army was called in with flamethrowers, which worked splendidly!

One poignant incident left a strong impression on me. An elephant named Moni worked in the programme with us. One day in Stockholm, Moni's trainer Helmut commented that some of the bread that he occasionally fed the elephant to supplement her hay feed was missing. This disappearance of the bread went on week after week. Helmut finally decided he had to get to the bottom of it, so one evening after the performance was finished and Moni was bedded down for the night, instead of going back to his living quarters, he chose a spot in a corner of the stable, out of sight. Then he turned off the lights and made himself comfortable, waiting hopefully for the thief to show up.

Sure enough, a while later someone lifted the canvas side walling of the tent and crept in. Just as the person was about to grab the loaves of bread, Helmut pounced. He was surprised to discover that the person he had just wrestled to the ground was one of the young girls in a troupe of trapeze artists who performed in the circus.

"Micha!" Helmut cried out in disbelief. "But why?" In tears, Micha explained to Helmut that to keep their showgirl figures, their parents had put them on such a strict diet that they were always hungry – so much so that they were driven to taking the bread.

Helmut was a kind-hearted person and, from that time on, rather than turning in the thieves, he secretly gave the girls a regular supply.

*

Even before leaving England, I had begun to wonder about a career for myself. It never entered my mind to learn the family's dog act, so for the time being I resigned myself to following Dad around. It was 1963 and I had had my sixteenth birthday just before leaving Munich, but the turmoil I felt about what to do with my life was put to rest in Gothenburg when I first saw the incredible expertise, control and care with which the Schumanns trained and presented their horse acts. The Schumann family was composed of two brothers, Max and Albert, and their wives and children. It was Max and Albert who, apart from being the directors of the circus, did all the horse training.

I fell in love with the idea that one day I could be like them. If one saw circus as the gaudy, low end of entertainment, then this was the "opera" of circus. From that moment on, I wanted to be a horse trainer.

After Stockholm, the circus moved to Copenhagen for the summer months. We found an apartment in the main street (Vesterbrogade), about five minutes' walk from the magnificent circus building situated near the Tivoli. It was to become one of the happiest times of my life. We were all together as a family, our act was going well, and I was privileged to witness a standard of horse training that has become rare in the world of circus.

I made sure I was always present for the training, which took place early each morning. There was something majestic and noble about the way the Schumanns handled their horses. One could sense the mutual respect between horse and man – it reminded me of the way Dad was with the dogs. These were early observations that gave me my own basis for training animals. One of the main rules I learned was to have at least as much respect for the animal one is training as one expects to receive from the animal.

In the early morning, long before any crowds arrived to see the performance, the circus building was quiet inside. With its high cupola dome above the ring, it had a cathedral-like atmosphere. The first horses to be exercised were the ones who were "at liberty". These were a group of four to twelve horses that performed routines consisting of changing formations, but without any rider to guide them. The only sounds were the rhythmic breathing of the horses and soft treading of their hooves on the sawdust-covered ring. There was no loud whip cracking or any shouting. Mr Schumann stood in the middle of the ring, directing the horses. As I observed from the shadows of the auditorium, it was apparent that a quiet, dignified order prevailed.

As I watched them, I could feel the concentration of each of the horses as, with ears pricked forward and eyes alert, the group trotted round the ring, waiting for the slightest movement from Mr Schumann that would mean a command to change direction or make a pirouette. Sometimes, almost in a whisper, he called a name – Araby or Kismet – and the animal would come to him in an instant. Without fear, he stood obediently in front of him until given a tidbit, which Mr Schumann took from a leather pouch fixed to his belt. Then the horse rejoined the others, effortlessly finding his designated place in the group.

Early-morning rays of sunshine penetrated through small windows at the base of the dome structure, adding shafts of golden light that took on the role of spotlights. As the horses were put through their paces, sweat began to form on their necks and flanks. The smell of the sweat, the leather harnesses, the mustiness of the building and the occasional dung droppings churned into the fresh sawdust by the steady tread of hooves complemented the visual scene to cast a spell over me that made me forget all else.

While the training of the horses at liberty, who did various routines comparable to formation dancing, was fascinating to behold, what interested me the most was the "high school" or dressage riding, of which the Schumanns were masters. Observing them performing these skills ignited a strong flame of interest in me. *If I could learn to ride and train horses to such a high standard, my life would be complete*, I thought to myself.

Sometimes, while I was watching the Schumanns, they needed an extra hand, so they asked me to do little jobs, like leading the horses from the stables to the ring. Later on, when there was an opening for a groom, I volunteered for the job and ended up with six Lippizaner stallions to look after. They were my pride and joy and I made sure they were the cleanest horses in the stable. I wanted very much to stay on with Schumann as an apprentice horse trainer, but although I had a good relationship with them, they had their hands full teaching their own children and couldn't accept me as an apprentice.

But while my hopes of staying with Schumann had been dashed, my decision to be a horse trainer would not be swayed. After Dad completed two winter engagements in Paris and Rouen, we arrived back in Munich to start the summer season with Krone. With over sixty horses in the stable, the workload was enormous, and to help with the training and exercising of so many, Krone employed four or five people to receive tuition and become "bereiters" (assistant horse trainers). I was determined to become one and made myself as useful as I could in the stables. By the end of the season I was doing most all of the work the other bereiters were doing, but on a voluntary basis, with the promise of being taken on permanently the next year.

I left at the end of the season with Dad and Peter to join an Italian circus in Sicily for one month. Mother had left for a short break in England. When we arrived at the circus in Catania, it was late at night. The fence around the circus was closed, so we parked outside in the street. Just then a policeman arrived, and Dad was pleased to discover he spoke reasonably good English. He told us he learned English while a prisoner of war in England. Dad expressed his concern that we'd have to spend the night outside the circus ground.

"Don't worry," said the policeman, "my brother is in the Mafia – I will give him a call. He will see no harm comes to you." We therefore waited out the night with what was for us a most unusual brand of "protection"!

While we were with this circus, Winston Churchill died. The directors of the circus told Dad if he preferred not to work that day, they would understand. We were surprised so much respect was shown for Churchill, considering he had been their enemy during WWII.

There was another peculiarity of the circus in Catania that was worth noting: when the act was working, the ringmaster carried on a running commentary with the audience! He explained to them what was happening. We didn't think this was necessary for our act, because the visual way the act was constructed explained itself. But that was their style, and we couldn't do anything about it.

With our act, his commentary ran like this: "Be careful, Old Regnas, a dog is going to knock you down. Oh dear, it's too late!" And so he ranted on. Dad hated it, but his philosophy was, "When in Rome, do as the Romans do."

*

We returned to Krone for the next season and I continued my pursuit of becoming a bereiter. At the end of the season, my efforts were rewarded, and I was accepted as part of the horse-training team.

Mother, Dad, and Peter left Krone to join another circus, and for the first time I was on my own. I was seventeen. A compartment in one of the wooden circus wagons served as my living quarters, and I ate in the canteen with the rest of the workers. We worked incredibly hard. Our day started in the morning at eight sharp and finished at ten-thirty in the evening, with just short breaks in between. It was a time of mixed emotions for me: homesickness, living in a foreign country and excitement at finally embarking on my chosen profession. As it turned out, the nine years I spent with Krone were to be the only part of my professional life that had nothing to do with the family dog act.

Letters from Dad and the occasional phone call kept me informed of how things were going. Dad went from one engagement to another, seldom being out of work and usually only having enough time to get from one show to another.

In those days the celebrated American circus proprietor, John Ringling North, of Ringling Brothers and Barnum & Bailey fame, did an annual European scouting tour, looking for new acts. His character was admirably played by actor Minor Watson in the 1956 movie *Trapeze*, filmed at the Cirque d'Hiver in Paris, doing exactly that.

In 1967, when I was into my third year as an apprentice horse trainer, North came to see the Knie Circus in Switzerland, where Dad was working. He didn't waste time, and that very same evening invited Dad to his hotel to sign a contract for the next season for Ringling Brothers and Barnum & Bailey Circus in the US.

But just three months after we received the news of Dad's impending trip to the USA, everything changed. A phone call came from one of my uncles in England. I was called into Mr and Mrs Sembach's house, which was adjacent to the circus building, to take the call.

"Hello, Michael, this is your uncle Norman. I'm afraid I have some bad news for you."

I froze. Before Norman could continue, the thought flashed through my mind that someone had died – but who?

"We had a call from the Knie circus. I'm afraid it's your father – he died yesterday of a heart attack."

I was stunned. Dad was only forty-seven. To be eligible to work in Switzerland, he had had to undergo a medical check, and the result had given him a clean bill of health. I thought of Mother and Ma, and how they must be taking it. Mother was in England, so there hadn't been any of the family on hand at the Knie Circus with Dad. Knowing circus people, however, I at least felt sure someone would take care of Prince and Candy until we could get there.

The bosses of Krone, the Sembach family, were very kind and gave me immediate leave and some cash. I remember up until that point being a bit numb with shock, but on the drive from Munich to Zug, Switzerland, where the circus was, reality set in, and the sadness of Dad's death overwhelmed me.

The Knie Circus is very famous in Switzerland. They were, at that time, treated like royalty by everyone. Even in recent times, they continue to grab front-page headlines. Anything that happened at the Knie Circus was newsworthy, so when Dad died, it was no surprise to see headlines such as "The Death of a Clown". The funeral, which was arranged by the Knies, was an elaborate affair. The service was held in an English church in Bern, and representatives from the Knie Circus and the British Vice Consulate attended.

It was November and the Knie Circus had only one more month to go in their 1967 season. They asked either Peter or myself to carry on the act, but neither of us felt up to it. I was only nineteen at the time and didn't have a clue how to take Dad's place, not to mention that I was fully committed to my career as a horse trainer.

After the funeral, I brought Prince and Candy back with me to the Krone circus. One of the hardest problems to deal with was what to do with them. They were already quite old, so I didn't think they should be made to work any longer. To make things even more difficult, England had strict quarantine laws, which ruled out them being taken back to live with Mother.

I spoke to my bosses at the Krone Circus, but strangely, they refused my request to keep the dogs with me at the circus. If I'd been older and wiser I would have done otherwise, but as it was, I found homes for Barny and the dogs. I was young and made some foolish decisions, of which I'm now not proud. So, as I settled into my horse-training apprenticeship with the Krone Circus, an important chapter in the dog act's history came to a close.

*

The majestic and romantic aura of the Schumanns that had worked its magic on me for nine years hadn't faded. Horses were, and always would be, part of my life, but I'd sobered up to an ever-increasing responsibility towards Dad's memory and the act.

When I started working with Krone, it wasn't clear to me at the time, but I was just catching the tail end of an era in circus that had held the classical art of riding to a very high standard. However, things were changing. It had now been seven years since my dad died – the era of the seventies – fast food had arrived, and fast everything. The pace was also affecting the circus. Nobody had the time any more that was necessary to achieve perfection. With the exception of Fredi Knie Senior, who was one of the old school, the old masters of circus equestrian art on a par with Grand Prix Dressage were either dying off or retiring. The Schumanns had gone out of business and in the world of circus, their brilliant standard of horsemanship was now only history.

These events were influencing the way I was beginning to think. Somehow I had to earn more money. The salary with Krone was hardly enough to live on, and there didn't seem to be any prospect of that changing.

For some time it had played on my mind to have a go at reviving the dog act. In the years since Dad died, no one had tried to copy the act, which was very surprising, considering the success he had with it. There was no copyright covering the act, which left the door open for anyone to try. I made up my mind that at all costs, the act must stay in the family. Speaking to Peter about my thoughts, he agreed and gave his blessing for me to be the one to give it a try.

A lucky break presented itself in 1974, when I was offered a three-year contract in England to train and present horse and other animal acts. It made the perfect deal for my needs. The company's first engagement was to supply three animal acts for the summer season in the Hippodrome circus building in Great Yarmouth. Two other acts would be provided for me to perform with, and if I was ready in time the dog act would make up the third one. This opportunity meant I could finish my obligation to Krone and leave after the season finished in November. The dog act would have to be ready in May. It was a tight schedule, but to be signed up for work even before the act existed was almost too good to be true and worth the risk. It gave me a chance to jumpstart the dog act, which I intended to present, eventually, as my sole occupation.

The evening before my planned journey to the new job, I said goodbye to my friends at Krone. The next day I rose early. Munich is cold in November, and there was a frosty nip in the air as I made my way to the stable block to say the most emotional farewell of all. It was the same stable in which we housed Barny all those years ago when we first arrived from England.

Citro, a fifteen-hands-high Anglo Arab, stood calmly in his stall. It was too early for the main morning feed and he was munching away on leftover hay. Citro was the first horse I'd been given to train completely on my own, and I was very proud both of his abilities and the job I'd done in training him. When the circus was in Vienna, thanks to Circus Krone's excellent relations with the famous Spanish Riding School, we were able to attain the services of one of their expert bereiters to give us lessons. Five days a week from ten in the morning until noon, during our one-month stay in Vienna, our group of circus bereiters were instructed in the "Haute Ecole" of horsemanship. Up until our last day in Vienna, I had been riding two other horses during these lessons; I hadn't ridden Citro because I preferred to do my training with him early in the morning before the main training session began. I found the solitude helped me concentrate. Without distraction from other riders in the ring, I'm sure it helped Citro as well, and he was more attentive to my voice, leg and rein commands (called "aids"). But I didn't want to miss the opportunity of our work together being evaluated by such an expert, and on the last day of our instruction I rode him in the lessons. Our teacher from the Spanish Riding School pointed out a few mistakes that I hadn't been aware of, and then I saw him lean over to my boss, Christel Sembach, and whisper something in a low voice that I couldn't hear.

Later on, I was surprised to learn that he had confided in her that he was impressed at the high standard that Citro had attained and asked if I had trained him on my own. Of course I had, and I felt proud of my abilities, but it was also Citro's talent, his willingness to learn and our bond to each other that permitted such a successful outcome.

Now it was hard to say goodbye, but my future was beckoning. I stroked his muzzle and gave him a gentle pat on his muscular neck. I would miss him, but I had no qualms about his wellbeing. Circus Krone were exemplary in looking after their animals. I stroked him one last time, then made my way back to my living quarters opposite the circus building.

There, parked next to the wooden living wagon that had been my home for so long, was my most prized possession, a Lotus 7 two-seater sports car that I'd purchased second-hand. It was the one extravagant luxury I could afford – the whim of my youth. I didn't have much luggage, but what I did have was so tightly crammed into the car I could barely get my hand to the key to start the engine and put the car into gear. I started her up and set out along the deserted streets, headed back to England.

2

I HAD NO ILLUSIONS THAT TRAINING THE act and playing the role of Old Regnas would be anything but rigorous. The sequence of the tricks that made up the act were locked into my memory, but I hadn't any hands-on experience with training dogs. I was only eleven years old when Dad trained Candy and Prince. Accompanying him on his various engagements only gave me a chance to observe him correcting minor problems that cropped up in the dogs' routine. I wasn't sure I could remember how Dad trained a dog from scratch.

Then I thought about Citro, and my experience with him gave me confidence. In training what was called a "high school" horse, some movements require two people – a rider and another person on the ground. Because I was training Citro very early in the morning before the others started work, I had to devise ways to do everything myself, and in the end, my sometimes very unconventional methods were highly successful. Even if I couldn't remember all the little details about how Dad trained the dogs, I would rely on my own intuition. I felt confident I could find the right way.

In England, after spending some time with Ma in London, then Mother in Torquay in the south-west of England, and also visiting some other relatives and friends (sadly, by that time Uncle George had also passed away, though his voice lives on in the BBC archives as Roy Plomley's guest on Desert Island Discs) I settled into my new job. I was eager to get going and made the first tentative plans as to how I should begin to get everything ready for the act.

One positive thing the horse training had taught me, especially the German way, was to be systematic. The first thing I did was to write out a chart noting all the things I needed, starting with the dogs, the donkey, then the props, right down to what kind of boots to wear with the costume. That accomplished, I set about finding the first thing on the list – a big dog.

Every day I bought a local paper and scanned the classified ads under "animals for sale". After a week or so, something caught my interest. "Old English Sheepdog for sale, male – six months old." I telephoned and made an appointment to see the dog that evening.

All my endeavours concerning the act had to be done in between my horse work, so it was already dark when I found the house. A tall, thin man with black hair, somewhere in his thirties, answered the door.

"I've come about the ad in the paper."

"Ah, you must be Mr Freeman, come in." He showed me into the living room and introduced me to his wife. She was sitting on a sofa with her head bowed. Her hands clasped a white handkerchief. Not speaking, she just nodded her head to acknowledge me. It was then, with a twinge of embarrassment, I noticed her eyes were moist.

An impatient look flashed across the man's face. "The dog's out in the back," he said brusquely.

He led me through the house out to a shed in the backyard. It was a moonless night and pitch black outside except for the beam from a flashlight the man held. He opened the corrugated tin door to the shed and flicked on a light switch. A dog sat at the far end, a forlorn look about him as he blinked through his long hair at the harsh light from the naked bulb hanging from the roof. It was cold and damp inside, but it didn't seem to bother the man that these weren't ideal conditions in which to keep a dog.

He seemed very timid, which should have been a warning as to the dog's suitability for the act, but then again, this was new to me. I didn't have any idea what kind of personality I should be looking for. I would learn the hard way what type of dog is best suited to learn the routine of the act.

"I'll take him," I said. "By the way, what's his name?"

"Jake," said the man. He didn't bother to reassure the dog, so I took the initiative.

"There's a good boy, Jake," I said, trying to gain his trust. "Come on, let's get this lead on you."

I led him back through the house and gave the man the money. When the wife saw me holding Jake by the lead, she came over to him and stroked his head, a sniffle escaping as she said goodbye.

"I promise to take good care of him," I quietly reassured her.

Feeling I'd already established a bond with the dog, I led him to the Lotus. With his fringe of long hair cascading over his eyes and his tongue hanging out, it gave him a rather dopey look that made him all the more lovable. I sat Jake in the passenger seat. He looked terrified as we zipped along the country roads, his hair blowing straight back. For the first time, I could see his eyes.

I didn't like the name Jake very much, and decided to change it to Jaka. At six months, he was still only a puppy – too early to start training him. First we needed to get to know each other; above all, I had to gain his confidence.

*

During the time I began to work at building a bond with Jaka, I went about looking for a small dog for the act. After ten days, I still had no leads. Then I heard about a donkey for sale nearby.

The farmer who owned him wanted thirty pounds, which was a very fair price. It must have been my lucky day, because while I was looking at the donkey, I noticed a small white and brown Jack Russell terrier tied up on a long rope outside the stable. I asked his name.

"Patchy," said the farmer.

He was just the right dog for the act. I said, "If you throw in the dog, I'll give you the thirty pounds you're asking."

Obviously there wasn't much love lost between him and the dog, because without hesitation, he agreed.

On the way home with Patchy by my side and the donkey riding in the horse box I'd borrowed for the occasion, I realised I had forgotten to ask the donkey's name. But it didn't matter – whatever his name was, I'd rename him Barny, after Dad's faithful old donkey.

Now that I had the animals for the act, I started to assemble the props. They included two boxes, a cart, a chair and a big trunk for the finale, where Jaka would push me inside the trunk and close the lid on me. Then he'd proceed to push the trunk out of the ring, which was easier than it looked because I'd fixed wheels underneath.

I drew up another chart listing all the tricks that the dogs had to learn, noted in sequence. Alongside each trick I marked an approximate time in which I expected the dog to learn the trick, with the intention of teaching them each trick, one at a time, until the act was complete.

Before actually beginning the training, I took Jaka and Patchy to the training area and just played with them. Central to all animal acts of this nature, there must be a base from which to teach the tricks. Whatever methods of training I would think up myself, this was one traditional part of training the dogs I couldn't dispense with. To this end, after playing with them for some minutes to make them feel at home and comfortable in their future workplace, occasionally I would say, "Place," and lead them to a low pedestal then sit them on it. Then I'd make a fuss over them, to show them they had done well. It didn't take long for them to understand. Whenever I said, "Place," they went alone to the pedestal, which served as a kind of home base for them from which to carry out their separate roles in the act.

Things moved slowly at first, but as the dogs began to understand my gestures and words of encouragement, it had the effect of accelerating their learning capacity. Early in the training, I discovered the importance of improvising when problems arose. For example, Jaka had to learn how to knock down the boxes on command. I started by leading him from the pedestal to the upright standing box. Then, I would gently lift his front legs and place his paws on the side of the box, which would give way to his weight and fall over. At first it frightened him when the box fell away from him, and he started to shy away from the trick. My solution was to place the box against a solid wall until he gained enough confidence to put his full weight against it without the box giving way. Then each successive day I'd move it an inch or so away from the wall – and each day move it a little farther away. Because it was done gradually, he didn't seem to mind, and it didn't take long for me to be able to do away with the wall altogether.

Like Dad, I kept my training sessions short (ten to fifteen minutes) because I didn't want the dogs to feel it was a grind and make them unhappy, but keeping in mind the necessity of having the act ready for Great Yarmouth, I pushed it to the limit. We worked three sessions per day, with one day off in the week.

Periodically, I checked the chart hanging on my bedroom wall to see if we were keeping to schedule. Although Patchy had learned his relatively small part in the act (two tricks) fairly well, Jaka, on the other hand seemed slow in grasping things. I was afraid the act wouldn't be complete in time for Great Yarmouth.

Never mind, I thought. *We'll make do, and once the act is working I'll continue to train and slip the missing tricks in later.*

There was something I'd been avoiding for some time, but it was inevitable – I must sell my beloved Lotus and get more suitable transport. The Lotus was a real enthusiast's car and before 8am on the day I ran the ad in the paper, I'd already received ten enquiries. I sold it that same day for seven hundred pounds – the same price I paid for it. With the money from the Lotus safely in my possession, I began to look for something big enough to transport the props, Barny and the dogs. There were plenty of vehicles to choose from in the classifieds of the local paper, and I settled for a Bedford light utility van that was also strong enough to pull a small living trailer. At last, I had most of the items I would need to move from one venue to the next and proceed with the act.

*

Because the act had been a creation of my own family, I felt within my rights to keep the name of "Old Regnas", so that's how we were billed on the programme when, two weeks prior to starting in Great Yarmouth, we travelled with a small tent circus run by the French Santus family where I made my debut with the act.

The old-man makeup consisted of a large moustache glued on, some pencilled-in lines to make me look old and spectacles with clear lenses to complete my facial character. The costume was composed of a trilby hat (a soft felt hat with an indented crown), a neckerchief, a green apron, checked shirt, baggy pants and heavy oversized army boots.

We readied ourselves at the artist entrance near the back door. The music started to play, the curtain opened and I rode in on the cart pulled by Barny. He stopped in the middle of the ring and wouldn't budge. I tried to gee him on by flapping the reins over his haunches, to no avail. Everything was going according to plan and the public were already laughing. I stepped off the cart and, leaning my shoulder against Barny's backside, I tried to push him. He just dug his hooves in and still wouldn't move an inch forward. (More laughter.) I tried pulling him from the front, and this time he dug his hooves in the opposite way. To the public, Barny was one hell of a stubborn donkey – actually he wasn't; he'd just learned his stuff well.

Playing to the audience, I seemingly hit on the idea to entice Barny with a carrot. So, making a big display of giving him the carrot, I mounted the cart. Then, Barny, having received his reward, obligingly moved forward. I flipped a secret lever and the shafts connecting him to the cart broke away. The cart fell backwards and I took a fall. Barny then made his exit and Jaka came in and sat on the pedestal.

I noticed how he stared at the audience. I started to stack the boxes. Getting hold of the first one, I stood it end up and went to fetch the second one. With my back turned, this was the moment Jaka must come and knock the first one down – nothing. I lifted it up and plunked it down a second time. Still nothing. Jaka was glued to the pedestal, staring at the audience through his fringe of hair. I tried another couple of times and even went to the pedestal, trying to reassure him, but it was no good; he stayed frozen to his place.

I gave a sign to the prop boys standing in front of the curtained artist entrance to let Patchy in. Patchy did his part impeccably, jumping up onto my back as I pretended to tie my shoelace, and as I rolled backwards, over and over, he continued running across my shoulder and in between my legs, always managing to stay on top. The live performance didn't worry him a bit, and he was working exactly as he did in the rehearsals. Then I did my second trick with him. He threaded his way through my legs, in and out as I walked along. But I'd run out of tricks – there was nothing more to be done. I took my bow and made my exit to a stupefied public, who were probably thinking that that was a short act and wondering what the second dog was doing there. Jaka couldn't get out of the ring fast enough; he eagerly followed me back to our living trailer.

People were Jaka's problem. He'd been cooped up in that shed as a puppy, and since then had seen few people other than me. I knew I had a fight on my hands to reassure him and get him used to crowds. I had trained him in comparative seclusion at my boss's winter quarters, where we were more or less on our own. I'd underrated the difference between training and a live performance and was at a loss as to what to do.

The one person I thought could help me was Ma, but she had made a new life and home for herself in London, and shared an apartment with a distant cousin. She was touching eighty now, and I didn't want her to have to travel to me and endure the rigours of this small travelling show. Nevertheless, I needed her advice and phoned her up, speaking at length about the problem with Jaka. She told me she and Dad also had a problem getting Prince used to the public (I hadn't been aware of this) and I would just have to have patience and persevere.

I took Jaka for walks in the town. I sat with him in parks, watching the people go by, and talked to him to try to give him confidence. Whenever I rehearsed with him in the empty tent, he did all the tricks that he'd learned, but in the actual live performance, he wouldn't move from the pedestal, and I was still getting by with what Barny did and Patchy's small contribution. In this circus, the management didn't seem to mind that the act wasn't up to standard, but I knew it would be different at the Hippodrome Circus in Great Yarmouth, which had a reputation as a serious tourist attraction that engaged international circus stars.

The days passed quickly, and the short time with the little circus was drawing to an end. On the last day, I managed to coax Jaka off the pedestal to do something. It wasn't really a trick but gave some kind of plausible ending to the act, where I chased after him, running round the ring. The intended finale to the act should have been when Jaka pushed me into the big trunk, but I hadn't even begun training for that. This improvised finale, of him running round the ring with me chasing him, was better than nothing, and he really enjoyed doing it – his little stub of a tail wagged furiously. So I thought maybe a fun thing like this might merge into the other parts of the act and jerk him out of his frozen stupor.

*

When I first entered the Hippodrome circus building, the wooden construction and the smell of greasepaint and sawdust reminded me of the old Lorensberg Cirkus building in Gothenburg, Sweden. If the act was on a par with Dad's, I could almost imagine myself slipping into his boots. Nevertheless, feeling a touch of nostalgia, I vowed to make myself worthy to carry on his good name, and on opening night I said a silent prayer that Jaka would move away from his fear and knock the boxes down.

When time for my act arrived, I was hoping for the best as I rode in on the cart. What would I have done without Patchy and Barny? As usual they worked well, but when I placed the box down and walked away, and Jaka didn't move; my heart sank.

The difficulty in the dog act, and also something that made it different from other acts of its kind, was that the dogs had to work on their own with split-second timing. The theme of the act was the mischievous things they did to me. So, if I had to turn round and coax Jaka to come away from the pedestal to knock the box down, it defeated the storyline.

Poor Jaka's behaviour was ruining the act, but I knew he could do it, and somehow I must find a way to overcome his reluctance in front of an audience. A week went by with no appreciable improvement. Things came to a climax when I went to the management to offer an apology for our poor performance.

Mr Roberto Germains, who was also an artistic agent, said, "I must admit I have thought about pulling the act out of the show, but then one morning I saw you rehearse with the dogs. I could see the big dog was capable of working fairly well, so I have decided to give you one more week to improve things."

I didn't take this conversation at all to be a sign of retribution; on the contrary, I thought he was being very lenient with me.

Several days passed and I was still racking my brain to find a solution without much success. I had no illusions that this night would be any different from any other. True to my expectations, when I put the box down, Jaka still sat sullenly on the pedestal. I moved away, praying as always that he'd carry out his work, but not holding out much hope.

At that moment, "Crack! Crack!" came a noise like two explosions from behind the curtain. Two seconds later, from the corner of my eye I saw the box go flying through the air and land about three yards away from where I had put it. I looked in amazement at Jaka, who was already sitting back on the pedestal with an expression of alertness about him that I had never seen before.

This entire sequence of events took me so by surprise that I forgot what I had to do next – we'd never taken the act this far before! I quickly pulled myself together. Foregoing the normal routine that was supposed to follow (which should have been me tripping over the fallen box as I tried to stack the second one on top), I went over to Jaka and made the biggest fuss over him, showering him with caresses and saying, "Good boy, good boy," and assuring him that he had done well.

Realising I was still in front of an audience who were most probably expecting some more action, I got on with the rest of the routine. This included Patchy's bit of jumping onto my back and running through my legs as I rolled over backwards. Incredibly, Jaka did all the other tricks that he had learned up to that point perfectly – like pulling a chair away just as I was about to sit on it, and the trick where we sit on opposite ends of the cart and we play see-saw until he suddenly jumps off when I'm at the top of the movement, causing me to take a fall. We also did some other slapstick comedy, right up to the finale where I chased him round the ring.

When we got out of the ring, I again showered encouragement on Jaka, petting him and giving him plenty of verbal praise: "Good boy, good boy!"

I could never have imagined that the problem with Jaka would be resolved in such spectacular fashion. What had occurred was that that night, there was a change in the sequence of acts in the show, and a whip-cracking act that normally worked much later in the programme instead followed the dog act. Normally, I'd have thought how stupid and thoughtless of the next performer to crack his whips while another act was working. As it turned out, his timing was impeccable.

Whip cracking is not part of my training methods, and what happened there was entirely unexpected. But I still like to think it was some divine intervention in answer to my prayers. Of course, until the next performance, I couldn't be sure if Jaka's new zest in working wasn't a fluke. He might go back to his old ways. However, the next evening, he didn't wait for any whip to crack. He knocked the box down right on cue (only it didn't fly quite so far this time)!

From that moment on, Jaka gradually improved and at last I was able to concentrate more on playing my role. The act began to make sense to the public. To say we became an instant success would be an exaggeration, but the act did gain a sort of mediocre quaintness about it, if not for anything else than its difference from traditional dog acts.

Jaka began to develop a style of working that was quite appealing, insofar as he did everything in a deadpan sort of way, with clockwork precision. I knew, however, that he really wasn't the best dog for the act. To fulfil the overall character and complement the storyline, the act needed a lively, happy dog – one with "pepper". Furthermore, if I was going to make the dog act my future, I couldn't take the risk that Dad did in having only Prince as the one main dog for the act with no backup, so I set about looking for another dog.

*

I let a few people know I was on the lookout for a new dog, including one of the "prop boys" – a man named Ricky. He also did odd jobs around the circus. Ricky was one of those people whom you couldn't help but like; he had such a happy attitude towards life. If tensions were running high or if anyone was dismal and down, he always made things seem better.

One morning I was rehearsing with one of the horse acts I was presenting when I heard Ricky's voice calling my name. "Mike, look what I've got for you."

I turned round to see Ricky standing in the opening to the ring. By his side was a black and brown dog with a bandaged leg. He was a medium-sized dog and rather looked like a large border collie. For a moment I just stared. Ricky proceeded to tell me that a minor driving licence problem that morning had taken him to the police station. While he was there, some officers came in with the dog. Ricky loved dogs, so he asked the officers how they came by him. They said he was a stray; unfortunately, after they picked him up, as they were driving along, he jumped out of the open window and injured his leg. They took him to the local veterinary clinic to be treated before bringing him in to the police station. Their intention then was to take him to the pound. Ricky asked if he could take charge of the dog and find him a home. The police agreed, and he brought him straight to me.

I looked the dog over. He gazed back at me with sharp, intelligent eyes, as if silently trying to provoke a response from me. In comparison to Jaka's lovable but timid and slow character, I could sense this dog had a vibrant energy just itching to get going. It was love at first sight, and I knew I'd found my new dog. Without even considering other names, I called him Prince.

On reflection, while writing about the evolving history of the act, I can't help but believe in fate, because a few days after Jaka's breakthrough, Mr David Smart from the Billy Smart Circus (the biggest one at that time in England) came to see the performance, accompanied by a BBC TV producer. He also knew Dad's act from years before. After the show, they came looking for me. I thought it was for old time's sake, because Dad had worked for both of them, but after greeting them and an exchange of small talk, Mr Smart posed a question that caught me by surprise.

"Would you like to do our Christmas TV show?" he asked. Objections raced through my mind. I felt it was happening too fast and I wasn't ready for something big like that, but, after stammering "um" and "er" for what seemed like ages, common sense gave my thoughts a shove and I choked out, "Yes."

"It needs polishing up a bit, but we both liked your dad's act. After speaking to Roberto, he thinks you've worked hard and done a good job, considering the short time you've worked with the new dogs. We feel sure you can improve the act in time for November when we televise the performance."

This was the same TV show that had catapulted Dad's act onto the international circus scene – the difference being that Dad's act was already a success when they televised it. I began to wonder if I'd jumped the gun a bit in accepting the offer. If the act wasn't up to standard when seen on TV it might ruin my chances of getting booked later. After agonising about this for some time, I decided it was worth the risk and redoubled my efforts to make the act better.

Soon after acquiring Prince, an unfortunate incident occurred when I took him to the veterinarian for a checkup on his injured leg, and to have the bandage removed. When we arrived at the clinic, Prince was his usual bouncy self, full of confidence and happy with life. However, while we were waiting to be ushered into the consulting room, an awful change came over him. I'd never seen him in this state before. He was shaking and staring straight ahead and wouldn't respond to any effort to calm him. I dismissed it as a severe case of not liking veterinarians, but nothing could prepare me for the veterinarian assistant's attitude.

"What have you been doing with that dog?" she asked in an aggressive tone.

"Nothing," I replied.

"You're from the circus, aren't you? Have you been hurting him? He wasn't like this last week when the police brought him in."

I tried to suggest maybe he was afraid of the vet.

"That can't be true," she said. "When he was brought in a week ago by the police, he didn't behave like this."

I was at a loss as to how to combat her obvious mistrust of me as a dog owner. Slowly, Prince calmed down somewhat. His leg was given the okay by the vet, who thankfully dismissed the incident with a shrug of his shoulders. But as we left, the assistant looked at me with suspicion and disgust. At that moment I felt the whole weight of the distaste and disregard that some people have for circus people with performing animals. The fact that I was completely innocent made me feel even worse, but I didn't know what to say to defend myself.

The problem with Prince remained a mystery until about a year later, when I discovered the real reason for his behaviour. We were with a circus in France that was situated next to a police dog training centre. To get the dogs used to all types of situations, they fired shots. When this happened, Prince went into the same trancelike state as before, shaking all over, and I couldn't communicate with him. But it was even worse than at the vets in Great Yarmouth, and it took him a whole day to get over it. I can only assume that the first incident was triggered by some bang that I wasn't aware of at the time – maybe a car backfiring in the distance. I never

found out, but it was confirmed on at least three other occasions –
for example, at new year celebrations when fireworks went off. On
those days the terror from bangs gripped him and doing the act
with him was out of the question.

*

Apart from the other two animal acts I presented for the
Hippodrome, the dog act consumed my life. My days consisted
mostly of training the dogs, seeing to their needs, tinkering with
the props and thinking about how to make the act better. One little
detail I came up with early on was to replace the wooden boxes with
baskets, which a local craftsman made to my own specifications.
I made this change because the wooden ones were too solid and
wouldn't give when being thrown about and knocked over, so they
had started to break up. The woven baskets, on the other hand,
were better suited because they were more flexible.

With two months to go before the season finished at the
Hippodrome, Jaka had learned the trick for our finale in which he
pushes me into the big trunk case, closing the lid, and then pushes
the trunk with me inside it out of the ring. Of course it wasn't Jaka
pushing the whole weight of the trunk and me. Thanks to a false
bottom, I was able to get my feet to the ground and pushed us
along. Jaka only had to rest his paws on top of the trunk and follow
along with his hind legs. It just looked as if it was him doing the
work.

When I began to train Prince, the difference between my first
efforts at training him and Jaka was incredible. Prince was a bundle
of energy; he was so fast in his movements I could hardly keep up.
Although Jaka was working reasonably well, I had to work at a slow
pace for him and sometimes coax him a little. With Prince it was
the opposite – I had to slow him down. Sometimes he arrived at
the basket to knock it down even before I'd moved away. With Jaka,

and subsequent dogs I've trained, I usually have to fake it and take a dive as they hit me in the back; not so with Prince. He hit me so hard with his paws that, even if I wanted to, I couldn't stay upright. It was exciting to work with Prince and I couldn't wait to debut him in the performance, but I forced myself to be patient. Prince would be the act's passport to real success, and I didn't want to jeopardise that by training him too quickly. I always remember one of Ma's sayings: "Quick to learn, quick to forget."

Right from the beginning, I wanted the dogs to live with me as pets to gain the bond and understanding between us that would help me in their training. Now that my dog family was growing, I needed to keep everything under control and not provoke any jealousy between them. Fighting amongst themselves was something I could not tolerate. Patchy was a Jack Russell, a breed well known for its fearless courage and instant readiness to pick a fight, so I had to be extra careful. In the beginning, there were a few scraps between him and Jaka, but after intervening each time, and exerting a touch of discipline, things quieted down. I took the dogs out four times a day for walks, and other than that, we lived together in my trailer – which posed a problem sometimes with girlfriends!

One time, I invited a girl to my trailer. Patchy was in one of his jealous moods and kept eyeing her suspiciously. During the evening I had to check on Barny, who was in the stable with the other animals. I returned with high hopes of advancing my amorous intentions, but there was no sign of the girl. I thought maybe she'd changed her mind about me and left. Then I saw Patchy standing guard by the bathroom door. I opened the door to find the poor girl inside. She wouldn't come out until Patchy had been removed. Apparently, after I left the trailer he had become very menacing towards her, forcing her to take refuge in the bathroom. The episode killed any romantic atmosphere there might have been, and when the girl left, Patchy looked undeniably triumphant.

My act was still nowhere near as good as Dad's had been; however, after the season finished in Great Yarmouth, I felt we'd accomplished more than I had hoped for. The act wasn't fantastic, but we were good enough to secure work for the coming winter season, which included the TV show.

When the time came to do the televised show, I was extremely nervous but resolved to give it my best and prayed the dogs would do likewise. In those days the BBC crew, under a certain Mr Davis, were probably the most professional team at televising circus – in Europe, anyway.

I was especially grateful to the makeup girl, who showed me how to enhance my old-man look. I was born into this business but certainly no born artist. In fact, I was very frightened of working in front of an audience. In those early days, my costume consisted of a large moustache, a wig, glasses and hat to hide behind. Also, it was my objective to have the dogs so well trained that I could use the audience's appreciation of them as an added cushion between me and the public. However, that was detrimental to the act, because I should have played my role just as well and with equal enthusiasm as the dogs. It's funny that I had learned to be picky about what kind of dog is right for the act. If it had been the other way round, and the dogs had to choose their human partner to complement the act, I think they would have passed me by:

"Oh, no, not that one – he's kind and lovable, but much too timid."

The time for the TV show came, and I was reasonably pleased with how we worked. After that we had some time off.

Our next engagement after that was in Manchester in the north of England, still working under my existing three-year contract from 1975 to 1977 and presenting the same acts.

The two other animal acts I had presented in Great Yarmouth, and would be presenting in Manchester along with the dog act, fell under the category of "liberty" acts, in which animals – often very large animals – respond to verbal commands and signals and perform various routines and tricks free of ropes, leads or any physical contact with the trainer. The first act comprised three camels, three zebras and three ponies. One of the tricks we performed went like this: all the animals began by circling the ring, to music, of course. Then I called the three camels into the centre of the ring, where they mounted their front hooves on three pedestals placed in a row. Then the ponies and zebras, who had continued to circle the ring, changed their formation and proceeded to trot in between and around the camels, tracing figure eights.

The difficulty in training and presenting this act was catering to three different species, each of which had its own particular character traits. A camel is a very aloof and, in my view, a very proud animal that doesn't like to be hurried if it doesn't feel like it. The zebras, on the other hand, were very flighty and prone to a nervous disposition – a natural part of their survival instinct, in which they must react quickly and use speed as their defence against being taken by a lion or leopard. It required a lot of careful handling to keep them at a steady pace that matched that of the camels. The ponies' dispositions were somewhere in between those of the other two species; they wanted to run faster than the camels, but they were not as nervous as the zebras.

The second animal act I was presenting was what is called in the profession a "Big and Little Act". It consisted of a Giant Shire horse which stood about seventeen hands high (five feet six inches) at the withers, and a tiny Shetland pony. The pony ran circles underneath the large horse's belly. The Shire's name was Sam, and the Shetland was Johnny. Giant Sam had a gentle, lovable character but the little pony was quite cheeky and sometimes nipped at Sam's legs as he passed underneath. My initial work training horses gave me the skills I needed to be able to pull off these acts with animals of very disparate personalities.

While I was working in Manchester, an offer came to send me with all the animals to Cirque Jean Richard in France. Jean Richard was an actor who was famous for his portrayal of the detective Maigret in a popular French TV series. He loved circus to such an extent that just remaining an ardent fan wasn't enough – he had started his own circus. I was told the dog act could be included in the contract, if I so wished.

Now I had to make a very big decision. The dogs had become a part of my life, and I felt a strong responsibility towards their well-being and their future. I never thought of them as a commodity and just objects with which to earn money. I wanted them to be able to spend the rest of their lives with me regardless of what might happen to the act. I considered them my family, and I knew if I left England with the dogs, I couldn't come back again. At that time, England had very strict quarantine laws – cats and dogs entering the country had to be sequestered in quarantine away from their owners for six months. For me, at that time, those strict quarantine laws were like the Berlin Wall. I never thought they would come down – it was one of those things that one thinks will always be.

The quarantine laws had been put into effect to guard against rabies entering England. Yet in all my subsequent years in continental Europe, I have never seen one case of domestic rabies. When Dad left England for the first time, there was a loophole in the law that allowed working dogs to come back to England. In fact, he did come back to work in a Christmas show in Glasgow, Scotland. But there were restrictions. A man from the Ministry of Fisheries and Food met Dad at the docks when he arrived from Ostend, Belgium, and accompanied him on his journey to make sure Dad kept the dogs on leads and under control at all times. Dad had to pay all the man's expenses for his return trip, including an overnight stay. The tough controls continued while Dad was at the circus building, and the dogs had to stick to a designated exercise area. Inspections were carried out once a week to check on compliance.

In the following years, other dog acts, not keeping to the

rigorous rules, abused this compromise in the law, so it was changed and the exception for working dogs was lost. Because this happened later, when Dad was already back on the continent, he wasn't confronted with the decision I now had to make in 1975.

Agreeing to go to France would, in all practicality, make me an exile for life from my country. I simply couldn't bear the thought of my dogs being shut up for six months. I'd heard stories of the dogs who did make it through the whole six months and were often never the same again. Some of the kennels used for quarantine exploited the quarantine law and were only out to make money. They charged a huge amount, yet the dogs were not well cared for. (Fortunately, thanks to the efforts of some very influential people who were themselves returning dog owners, the quarantine laws were finally relaxed in 2001.)

I love England, and I will always think of myself as English, but after some thought, I couldn't ignore this opportunity. I had to follow wherever work was offered, so I agreed to go. I was twenty-eight years old when, together with the dogs and Barny, I took the boat to Calais, France.

As I stood on the stern and looked across the churning, frothy white wake of the ship, watching the white cliffs of Dover recede into the distance, my feelings were a mixture of sadness at leaving my country and of excitement at what might lie ahead.

*

Make no mistake – the old-fashioned tales about the circus being a world of glitz and glamour may not be entirely true, but it still has a particular mixture of raw adventure and excitement that no other way of life can compare with. Because the dog act is central to this book, and so as not to confuse the issues surrounding it, I should not deviate too much – but there are countless untold stories that run parallel to it.

To live and work in a travelling show, sometimes visiting a different town each day, yet be living in a close-knit community of artists of many different nationalities, is an eye-opening experience. We had to deal with culture shock, trying to learn different languages and sometimes dealing with physical hardship. A freelance act such as Dad's dog act never knew where the next work offer would come from. He could be finishing a contract in Scandinavia, then have just a few days to travel down to Sicily for another engagement. Our mode of travel was overland; we had to rough it on the road, passing through all the different countries and cultures as we went. This was an exciting way to live, and I hoped to make the act good enough to attract multiple offers, so I had the opportunity to choose the most exciting place to travel to.

At this time, working with Jaka was much more reliable than it had been during those first few weeks in Great Yarmouth, where I was never sure if he'd turn up for a trick. After a couple of rehearsals at the Cirque Jean Richard, I felt comfortable in starting the new season with him. That way, I didn't have to push Prince in front of an audience before I thought the moment was right.

I discovered something soon after commencing work at Jean Richard: the dog act had been accepted with the contract on a trial basis! Apparently the management had engaged me because of the other acts I was presenting, which they had seen and approved of. But before I arrived, the dog act was unknown to them. It was made clear to me that if the dog act wasn't good enough, it would be pulled from the programme. As it turned out, we must have acquitted ourselves well enough because, just as in Great Yarmouth, we were kept in the show.

Prince's debut in a live performance could be regarded as either a success or a failure, depending on which way you looked at it. In one way, it was a disaster – he ran out of the ring after doing only two tricks! However, I knew the potential was there for him to lift the act to a much higher standard. I must admit, however, that at first I was very worried. The changeover from dry rehearsals to a live performance with the dogs was always a problem.

I phoned Ma once again, and she pointed out that Dad had had a big advantage over me, because he started the act at our own circus, which allowed him to make as many mistakes as he liked without fear of having the act pulled from the show. It also meant he could even stop the act if necessary and start over. I didn't have that luxury. If I didn't keep more or less to the given length of the act, I'd be in trouble with management. Thankfully, with Prince I needn't have worried so much, because in only a few days he was comfortable with the crowds, and in no time was working as well as he did during rehearsals.

Since adopting Prince, there was one obvious thing that stood him apart from Patchy, and especially Jaka: his extreme focus on me. My love for Jaka was mutual, and he definitely sought my affection, but I think he'd have preferred me to be a woman. Whenever he had a chance meeting with a woman, he would perk up and his little stub of a tail wagged at high speed. Prince, on the other hand, was a one-man dog. His attention was wholly on me, which made working with him a pleasure. His piercing eyes focused on me, as if to say, "What's next, what's next? Come on, let's get going!" His whole being seemed to shout out, "I want to please you," and he did everything with high enthusiasm. The difference between Jaka and Prince, in terms of their working ability and spirit, can be likened to the difference between a carthorse and a thoroughbred racehorse, or a Jeep and a Ferrari.

Just as I had predicted, with Prince as my partner, the act began to take off. Strangers complimented me on the act (that is, if they recognised me out of costume and makeup). I also noticed that some of the staff would slip into the tent just before the act was due to go in. Ticket sellers, office staff and even some of the management took prime vantage points. At first I didn't think they had come just to watch the act, but often, after I'd made my bow, acknowledging the applause, and we were making our exit, I noticed them already making their way out again.

Then, to top this newly established high that the act was experiencing, my friend and future agent, Mr Germains from England, informed me the Krone Circus management had seen me on TV and wanted the act for next January.

I was ecstatic! They had only seen the act with Jaka. *Wait until they see Prince*, I thought.

Unfortunately, Dad had been weak in his business dealings, and others took advantage of his good nature. Also, the circus artistic agents that Dad dealt with didn't help him much in this matter. They always told him to go for the lowest price possible. Dad was too good-hearted to offend anyone and always agreed to whatever was offered.

Previously, my salary had been linked to presenting the other acts and was a fixed sum wherever I worked. Now, for the first time I had to name an independent salary for the act, and I didn't want to make a mistake. While working in Great Yarmouth, I'd gained Mr Germain's respect and I trusted him to be fair with me. He was different from the agents Dad had to deal with, and I took his advice on how much money to ask for. When I was finally sent the contract to sign, Mr Germain's negotiations on my behalf earned me more than seven times my previous salary! To say I was delighted would be an understatement. All our efforts seemed to be proving worthwhile: not only was I doing something I loved, I was also going to be well-paid for it.

Towards the end of the season with Cirque Jean Richard, my life with the act had stabilised. Jaka had improved to a level that gave me even more confidence in working with him, and Prince's work was just fantastic. Patchy and Barny were also very reliable. Not having a backup for either Barny or Patchy made it necessary for them to work in all performances, but because they didn't have so much to do in the act, it was okay for them and not tiring. I used Prince and

Jaka alternately, with Jaka working in the afternoon performance and Prince in the evening. That way, it wasn't overly stressful for either of them and enabled me to keep Jaka in practice as a backup.

Because the timing of the tricks or gags that made up the story of the act had to be coordinated with the dogs, working one show with one dog and the next with the other kept me on my toes mentally. In the afternoon, I had to work slower and the act sort of plodded along at Jaka's pace, which kind of made it cute. In the evening, it took on a different character. With Prince's explosive energy and keenness to do everything just right, he put vibrant life into each individual trick, making it look natural, as if he hadn't been trained for it. Everything appeared to be some spontaneous idea of his own. He was the most natural-looking trained animal I have ever seen, and I was extremely proud of him.

Now, if only I could play my role as well as he plays his, I thought.

*

I began looking forward to my short winter season in Munich, where I could show off what we had achieved to my former horse-training colleagues.

When I was an assistant horse trainer, a bereiter, we were encouraged to think of ourselves as "house staff" as opposed to the upgraded rank of "circus artists". To arrive back at Krone as an artist in my own right with the act up and running gave me great satisfaction. In fact, being back in my old surroundings made me realise how much getting the act started had matured me, and I felt a newfound freedom and confidence in myself. Unfortunately, this new mood was dampened after I went to see Citro and found his stall occupied by another horse. With great sadness, I learned he had had to be destroyed after developing a bone disease.

I didn't let on about Prince to the Krone people straight away, and in the first few days of practice I just used Jaka. The dress rehearsal was scheduled in three days. The Krone Circus in Munich, with the exception of Cirque D'Hiver in Paris, the Hippodrome in Yarmouth and Carre in Amsterdam, is unique in Western Europe. It's one of the last bastions of traditional circus still taking place in a custom-made building, which was built in 1961 on the same plot of land as the old Circus Krone building had stood. To the eye, it takes on the same lines as a traditional European circus building, similar to the one in Gothenburg, only it was constructed with modern materials. The building, with its substantial stable annex, stands on its own piece of land only a few blocks away from the centre of downtown Munich. In the summer, when the circus is on tour, the building is used to host concerts of many different kinds of music, including rock. Although it wasn't large enough to house the huge crowds common for big stars, it is still used for smaller or more intimate concerts. The Beatles performed there in the sixties.

On the evening of the first show, I changed into my costume in the dressing room and left the building for the trailer park across the road to collect the dogs. When I opened the door, they came to greet me. Both of them knew something was up. They'd become accustomed to either one or the other going to work when they saw me in costume. I looked at them, contemplating for a moment as if undecided. Prince cocked his head to one side and pricked up his ears as he tried to read my intentions, then when I snapped the lead on him instead of Jaka, he started to wag his tail furiously.

I measured our success more in the dress rehearsal than in the actual opening night, because the audience was made up of staff, artists and some press people. A professional crowd is usually hard to get a reaction from, but we managed to grab their attention, and that really meant something. Those who were most surprised were the ones who had only seen me with Jaka. One of them, commenting on Prince's version of the act, said, "I see you played your ace tonight."

The reason I used Prince at Krone as often as I dared without tiring him was because I wanted the act to be seen in its best form as often as possible. When we were with the Jean Richard circus in France, we travelled a lot, which made it more difficult for agents or management from other shows to catch up to see the programme with the intention of booking new artists. In Munich, anybody who was somebody in the European circus world turned up scouting for new acts. Hardly a night went by without a fellow artist whispering in my ear, "Did you know so-and-so from so-and-so is in tonight?"

True, I had gained a lot of confidence, but I wasn't impervious to stage fright. The timing of the well-intentioned information that somebody important was in the audience usually came just before we made our entrance, which made me extra nervous. I'm sure the act lost some of its shine because of my edginess in front of the public, but my lesser performance didn't stop us from attracting enquiries about bookings from some of the best shows in Europe.

Realising how much I'd missed the horses, I stalled on the various agents' offers of work in hopes of securing a summer tour with Krone, where I thought I would feel more at home. However, one agent in particular was very persistent, telling me a well-known German circus wanted me for the following year. He came back twice trying to seduce me to sign a contract, but I was still holding out for an offer from Krone. He wouldn't give up and came back for a third try to persuade me, and he knew the right buttons to push.

"The boss of Circus Barum was very impressed with the act. He knew and admired your father, and he thinks you've done a good job. He'll pay you top money."

I didn't know what his idea of top money was. Normally in the protocol of such dealings, it's the artist who has to say how much they want for an engagement, but it appeared that my air of indifference on his previous visits had unintentionally given me the upper hand in negotiations. I hadn't purposefully played hard to get, but it was paying dividends because he seemed to be quite desperate to get me signed.

It was less a provocation on my part and more out of curiosity when I said, "Okay, how much?"

After hesitating for a moment, he mentioned a sum. I had to take a deep breath to stop from falling over backwards. Keeping to circus artist protocol, I will decline here to divulge the sum; suffice to say it was an offer I couldn't refuse.

I was looking forward to being free and on my own with the act like Dad was, but the circus I was with at the time, Cirque Jean Richard, had only given me leave from my contract for the Munich engagement and I was obligated to remain one more season with them, so the day after closing in Munich, I had to leave for France again.

*

When I arrived at Cirque Jean Richard's winter quarters in the city of Tours, France, I found a change had been made. The circus was expanding and a new unit of the circus had been formed. The other animal acts that I had been working were to stay with the original Jean Richard and be presented by another trainer, but the dog act was needed on the new show. Now I was still tied to my contract, but without the responsibility of the other animals, and that summer was unexpectedly easy for me. The dogs were working well, so there was no need to keep training them, and I began to experience a whole new way of life.

The route took us along the rugged Brittany coastline. Although the circus moved to a different town each day, the trips were short, and with only one performance per day, we had plenty of time for the beach and the seafood restaurants. We were living the life of tourists and getting paid for it!

When the conditions were right, I took the dogs swimming at the beach; I think they enjoyed it as much as I did, except I wasn't prepared for Patchy's antics. Sometimes when I was swimming, he swam up from behind and clawed his way onto my back. But still being partially submerged, he thought he had to make an effort to swim, and his continued leg movements made deep scratches in my back, which were made more agonising with the saltwater. Watching him swim alone was comical, with his small but muscular legs paddling away so fast; his little tail wagging at the back resembled a propeller, pushing him through the water like a miniature torpedo.

For all the good life, I didn't neglect the act. Although the dogs were fully trained and doing everything they needed pertinent to the routine, experience had taught me it was necessary to remain vigilant to any problems creeping in. To keep everything moving smoothly, now and again I had to make corrections. Mostly it was minor problems with timing, when the dogs would either come too early or too late for a trick. However, this kind of thing had to be put right fairly quickly or it could get out of hand and ruin the continuity of the act.

I still had to find winter work to bridge the gap we would have before starting with Circus Barum. The most enticing offer was to go to Rome for three months. It was before the relaxation of border controls in the European community, and there were strict laws concerning the importation of equines; this meant Barny needed a whole stack of paper forms from the respective agricultural ministries involving blood tests and temporary import permission. Each country had its own regulations so, to be on the safe side, I contacted the Italian embassy to make sure I would have the right paperwork and tests done in time.

The summer months drifted by and beach visits became fewer until finally autumn began to creep upon us and our route took us inland towards Paris. I was sorry when the season finished, knowing I'd be leaving behind friends with whom I might not meet up again for years. And I would miss life on the French circus. On the other hand, finally I was free with the dog act to go where I pleased, and what better start than to go to Rome for Christmas?

3

THE UTILITY VAN I HAD AT that time was beginning to be unreliable, so with good credit linked to my impending high salary with the circus Barum, I was able to buy a new Range Rover. I had the vehicle customised to accommodate Barny.

I planned to pass through Munich on the way to Rome, so I thought I would stay there for a while to finalise the paperwork needed for the animals to cross the border. I knew getting the dogs into Italy wouldn't be a problem; it was only England and Scandinavia that demanded more than proof of inoculations. But Barny needed various forms completed to be able to cross over.

Armed with all my properly filled-out ministry papers for Barny neatly arranged in a plastic folder, I felt pretty confident as I drove up to the Italian checkpoint at the Brenner Pass, high in the mountains. I gave the papers and my passport to the guard, and he disappeared inside the customs building. When he emerged a few minutes later, he told me a paper was missing, and without it he wouldn't let me pass. He said I needed a T-2 form or something like that – I don't remember exactly. And the only place I could acquire that particular form was in Munich, where the other papers had been issued. So I had to turn around and drive all the way back to Munich, where they gave me the T-2 form and said it shouldn't have been necessary.

After losing a whole day, I approached the Brenner border crossing again. Since it was early December, it was off-season, so there weren't many cars in front of me. I didn't have to wait long before I pulled up to the customs control and handed my papers to the guard. Like the day before, he disappeared inside. This time it was something different they found wrong, and I couldn't speak enough Italian at that time to understand what it was. I pulled over, parked out of the way and went inside the customs building to try to find out what the problem was this time.

The room was thick with cigarette smoke, and being a non-smoker, it required all my fortitude not to gag as I tried to argue my case in my few words of broken Italian. After a few minutes of discussion, I got the impression that the man I was confronting, as he sat smugly behind a long counter, couldn't care less if I came into his country or not. He was unshaven, his ill-fitting uniform was unbuttoned halfway down the front and his official-looking hat was askew in a slovenly fashion. His co-workers didn't look any better, giving the impression they had all just stepped out of a *Pancho Villa* movie.

After telling me of some obscure paper I needed, he suggested an alternative. He could issue me a special permit, but it would cost me five hundred thousand lira. I was too naïve at the time to realise he was asking for a bribe. But even so, I began to feel that I certainly was up against a load of bandidos. I felt very intimidated, lonely and frustrated by the situation. I didn't have that much money and told him so. In reply, he just hunched his shoulders and said I would have to wait until the veterinary inspector came some time, maybe tomorrow. He might give me permission to cross over then.

I drove away from the customs building and parked in no-man's-land between the two borders. It was freezing cold at night, but I had the dogs in the trailer with me for warmth. I made sure

Barny had plenty of straw under him and hay to eat. I fed the dogs, took them for a run and went to bed.

The next day, I went to see if the vet would be coming, and they said they didn't know. This routine was repeated for two more days, as I waited in vain for the vet. The situation was really starting to get to me, and I didn't know what to do. I was running out of food for the animals, so I decided to go find the veterinary inspector myself. But then I found that I couldn't, because his office was in the next village inside Italy! Driven by frustration, anger and a certain amount of fear at being stranded during mid-winter in the freezing weather, I made the incredible decision to unload Barny and tie him up to my living trailer. I left him standing there alone, while I drove off to find the vet's office. As I passed through the customs check without problems, I thought to myself, *I wonder if I could get away with smuggling Barny?*

I found the customs vet tucked away in his little office. He looked at my papers and told me the necessary negative blood test result for Barny should be on a separate form – not on the same paper as the other information. I asked him if it really mattered that much, but he was just as arrogant and unwilling to help as the customs man and refused to give way. Thoughts of Barny standing in the open on his own made me want to get back to him as soon as possible, so I left. I was glad to find him safe and sound. It was my fifth day on the border, and I was cold, hungry and really fed up. It was about 5pm, and I didn't want to spend another night there.

So I made the desperate decision to have a go at smuggling him. I knew I couldn't do it at the Brenner checkpoint; by then it was common knowledge I had a donkey with me. So I loaded Barny into the Range Rover, coupled the trailer up and drove back into Austria. They didn't give me any problems at all when I told them I was making my way back to Munich because of all the problems with the Italians. A few kilometres into Austria, I stopped and looked at the map. I decided to try my adventure at the Reschenpass, a little border crossing high up in the mountains that was also near the Switzerland border.

It was about nine in the evening when I got within ten kilometres of the Reschenpass. The road was very steep and twisty. I saw a secluded lay-by on the side of the road and pulled over, unhitched the trailer, got Barny out of the back door of the Range Rover and led him to the trailer. I opened the door and coaxed him inside with a slice of bread. At that time my living trailer had no separating walls inside except around the lavatory area. I led Barny through the trailer to my bed at the opposite end and tied the end of his head-halter rope to the supports of the bed. I gave him a reassuring pat and told him everything would be all right.

At the same time, I wished somebody would lay a hand on *my* shoulder, assuring me that everything would be all right. I didn't feel at all confident as to what I was about to do. Normally, as a law-abiding citizen I would shy away from something like this, but my back was against the wall and the Italian border guards (and perhaps the veterinary inspector as well) were obviously not going to budge without my handing out some generous bribes.

With the trailer hitched up again, I continued my way along the winding, climbing road. It had snowed, but the roads had been cleared and snow was piled along the sides. We encountered little traffic. As I approached the small border crossing, which I supposed was considered a tourist route, I thought, *There's no turning back now.* I pushed all negative thoughts from my head and drove straight up to the striped pole that blocked the road. I rolled down the window and made a big show to the guard on duty, waving my passport and the little booklets that carry each dog's inoculation details, hoping to draw his attention to one particular detail.

My strategy didn't work, and he insisted on having a look inside the trailer. I got out of the Rover, my bravado deserting me fast, and, with my heart in my mouth, opened the door. Ahead of the guard, I stepped inside. It was a little dark, but with the light from outside you could still see well enough. Without hesitating, I walked quickly to the end where Barny was tied to the bed. Luckily, he was in a straight line facing forward, and I quickly positioned myself to block the donkey from view. Barny is a small donkey, but his ears are enormous, and I was certain they'd be sticking up over my head, revealing to the border guard, as he arrested me, that I was indeed an ass! With my heart pounding, I clasped my hands together in front of me and pushed my arms back to my sides, trying to make myself as wide as possible. The guard stood where he was in the doorway, looking up and down the length of the trailer. He said something I didn't catch and stepped out. I let out a huge breath – I couldn't believe he hadn't seen Barny! I don't think I have ever felt so relieved and elated.

The guard returned my papers and, lifting up the striped pole that barred the way over the border, he even wished me a pleasant journey. I thanked him, got back inside and drove off as quickly as possible. You must realise that Barny is capable of braying at any time of the day or night, and I didn't want him to give us away now! After driving for some distance further down the winding descending roads, I stopped in a secluded spot and put Barny back in the Range Rover. Thankfully, he had had the decency to refrain from relieving himself next to my bed.

Shortly afterwards, I arrived in the first town and, to my horror, saw that everything was written in German: *Finckstrasse, Gastatte, Tageszeitung*. Horrified, I thought I must have taken a wrong turn somewhere and slipped into Switzerland rather than Italy – gone through all that trouble for nothing! Of course, I'm now admitting to my ignorance of geographical history at that time; I didn't know then that I was in the Sud Tirol, which, although part of Italy now, was Austrian in origin. The people still consider themselves Austrian and continue to speak German! It was another cold evening and quite late, so I was lucky to spot a couple walking along the otherwise deserted street. Barely daring to hope, I stopped and enquired as to what country I was in.

"Italy," they answered. I heard them laughing as I drove away. I didn't care that they thought it was funny; in fact, I even felt like laughing with them, I was so relieved and happy that after nearly six days of trying to get into Italy, we had finally made it!

*

While working with the Italian circus, I was happy to be allowed a brief encounter with horse training again. The family who ran the show had just spent a considerable amount of money to buy six beautiful Andalusian horses that had already been trained in Spain. Their plan was to start a high-school act with six members of the family riding them. The problem was nobody knew how to ride them properly. They welcomed my offer to teach them, and my efforts were such a success the proprietor of the circus wanted me to break my contract in Germany and stay to help them further. I felt flattered, but I didn't want to risk the good name of the act and start breaking contracts, so I declined the offer.

When the time came to travel back to Germany, I worried about getting Barny out of Italy. I started out on the journey with every intention of staying on the right side of the law and declaring him. However, when I found myself getting nearer the border, I couldn't escape memories of those many days being stuck there, and I knew I had to make some quick decisions. With no record of Barny coming to Italy, they would say I was exporting an Italian donkey. The road signs indicating the diminishing distance to the border were getting more frequent – "twenty kilometres", "ten kilometres". I had to make up my mind soon. Acting even braver than before, this time I didn't even bother to put Barny into the trailer. I just threw a blanket over him and continued to the little guard post. After rolling down the window, exclaiming, "Tourist!" and quickly flashing my passport, we were through in less than five minutes.

"*Phew!*"

A distance down the road I stopped and pulled the blanket off Barny.

We did the rest of the journey without a hitch, passing through Austria and on into Germany to the city of Wurzburg to start the summer season with Barum. It felt good being back in a country where I spoke the language fluently, and I settled easily into the life on the show.

Three months into the engagement, the act caught the attention of an agent scouting for acts to participate in the prestigious Monte Carlo Circus Festival. I signed a contract with them for the following winter.

*

That summer, 1978, we arrived in Bonn, at that time the capital of West Germany, so I could continue on with the Barum Circus. One evening after the performance, an impromptu barbecue was organised. The group had assembled in an open area just behind the British embassy. The previous day I had played cricket with some of the staff there. It reminded me of England and gave me a lot of pleasure. With Barum, the act was going well, and I felt generally happy with life.

The party began to wind down around midnight, and I decided to leave and give the dogs their last run before going to bed. I said goodnight to everyone and made my way to my living trailer. It was summer and a lovely evening. Since starting the act, I had settled into a predictable routine, with the first thing upon getting out of bed in the morning and the last thing at night, running the dogs. I did that from day one of starting the act, and I still do.

Upon reaching the trailer, I knew there was something wrong straight away because Prince, who was always very lively, didn't appear. Usually he would jump up and greet me when I returned. I have a sixth sense in situations like that and a shock went through me and a premonition as to what I might find. When I got inside, Prince was lying on the floor absolutely motionless. I knelt beside him and looked for any sign of life, but there were none – he had died. But he was still warm, and in a hopeless effort to do something, I tried to bring him back to life by cupping my hands round his nose and breathing into his lungs. Frantically, I tried that for some time until I knew it was no good. He was gone.

Everyone else in the circus had already gone to bed, so there was no point in arousing anyone. I lay Prince in the Range Rover and stayed with him for some time. It was the first time I'd experienced death first-hand, either human or animal, and I was devastated. In Great Yarmouth, the vet had put Prince's age at about six months. He was still so young, and I couldn't understand what could have taken him. I touched him one last time and noticed how his body was getting cold, then left to go to bed.

Back in my living trailer, I couldn't sleep and kept looking out the window, expecting to see Prince sitting up in the Rover looking back at me. Some time in the early hours, I did nod off to sleep, and I had a strange but wonderful dream in which Prince and I played happily together. The dream left me with a very strange feeling – haunted, melancholy, yet somehow believing that in some universe I had been able to have a last romp with my beloved Prince. The feeling stayed with me all day.

I arranged to have an autopsy done at a special veterinary clinic. Without any apparent reason for Prince's death, I wanted to know the cause so I could take precautions against it in the future for the other dogs. I wouldn't receive the results for several days.

For the next two days, everything seemed dull and empty. Prince had been the dog who had dramatically brought the act to life and helped carry it up to a level of professionalism that made it a favourite with audiences all throughout Europe. Prince had done his part with tremendous enthusiasm and precision, yet he had made it all seem spontaneous – he was a real star in every sense of the word. Prince would forever be in my heart and hold a place of honour in the history of the act.

I know now this feeling of loss is one of the sacrifices of living so intensely with the animals. We worked and played together, and the dogs suffered all the ups and downs of this life with me. They were my family.

German circuses are well organised. Barum had a very efficient press relations person named Pamela, and Prince's death made front-page news in the *Bild Zeitung*, a national newspaper. I liked Pamela and in a professional sense we got on very well together, so when she asked me if she could follow up the story of Prince with me going to the animal shelter the next day with some reporters to make a show of looking for a new dog, I said yes. At first I thought it was in bad taste, but Pamela was only doing her job, and that's why I agreed. But I was still mourning for Prince and in no mood to find a new dog, so I treated it purely as a publicity stunt.

*

In the meantime, I received the result from Prince's autopsy. It was written in technical medical terms, but what it meant was that Prince had had some kind of heart defect. I asked the vets whether they thought it had anything to do with the work, and they said it did not – he could have died at any time and there was nothing I could have done to prevent it. While relieved that I had not been the reason for Prince's death, I was still very sad at the loss of my loyal and loving friend and spectacular show partner.

I duly presented myself to the press office at nine-thirty the next morning, where I met the reporter and photographer from the *Bild Zeitung*. We all drove out to the dog shelter. It was like most animal shelters, with a reception building leading out to the dog pens. As I walked along the pathway, with the cages to the left and right of me, the photographer started taking pictures of me, so I made a half-hearted show of looking at the dogs.

Presently I came to a cage that housed only one dog. He had a medium-length coat, black with some tan, but I couldn't identify his breed. He was still only a puppy, but already the size of a German Shepherd. As I came to the cage, he came bounding up to the bars, wagging his tail. He licked my hand and tried to make as much of an impression on me as possible. Unexpectedly, hopeful, excited thoughts rushed into my head. However, I was grieving for Prince and I suppressed my excitement at this meeting. I carried on, with the cameraman clicking away. It took some time to cover all of the pens outside and when I had finished, I couldn't resist one more look at the friendly puppy.

This was a turning point.

If he'd come bounding up to the bars like before, it wouldn't have been such a big deal, but he didn't. As I approached, he just sat in the corner looking at me sadly, as if to say, "I tried my best when you came to see me the first time, but you just went on by. Now my chance has gone."

My heart went out to him, and I was hooked.

It was the start of a sixteen-year friendship. I named him Kelly. The animal shelter people said he was an Afghan mix, which I rather doubted. My instincts were proven true when one day, many years later, a gentleman introduced himself to me as the president of the Hovawart club. He had just seen the show and wanted to know where I had acquired my Hovawart. The gentleman inspected Kelly and said, "Yes, no doubt about it, he is a purebred Hovawart."

Apart from the sadness of losing Prince, I also faced a dilemma regarding what to do about my contract to go to Monte Carlo.

For the benefit of those who don't know, the "Festival du Cirque de Monte Carlo" is a competition with prizes for circus acts. The performances take place in the presence of a jury, two of whom, at that time, were Prince Rainier and his wife, Princess Grace.

Without my Prince, our hopes of winning a prize were now diminished. Everything depended on Jaka until Kelly was trained. After much thought, even without the prospect of a prize, I decided to go to Monte Carlo just for the fun of it.

Actually, not having the pressure of vying for one of the prizes freed me up to enjoy myself, and that's what I did. Also, I wanted to impress Mother with my newfound prosperity, so I invited her to visit.

In those days the heliport in Monte Carlo was right next to where the trailers were parked with hardly any dividing fences, and landings and take-offs were in full view from my trailer's window. To do things on a budget my intention was to take the bus to Nice airport where Mum would be arriving from London, then hop on a scheduled helicopter flight to Monte Carlo. After meeting up with Mum, we strolled over to the helicopter desk, where I was informed there were no more flights that day and all the helicopters had returned to their base in Monte Carlo. I was disappointed I couldn't carry out my plan and pleaded with the girl at the desk if somehow a solution could be found. She asked me to wait a moment so she could make a phone call. She made the call and, putting the phone down, turned to me and said if I paid the full hire price for the heli to do the two-way trip, it could be arranged. Now the big question was, how much is this going to cost, and I was almost too afraid to ask. But I really wanted to do this and so I went ahead with my question. "Six hundred francs," she answered, and I started to rummage through all my pockets and counted my loose coins; I had exactly six hundred francs. We took off and, being the only passengers, we could choose our seats to enjoy the view during the short flight. Jutting out into the sea like a peninsula, we passed over Saint Jean Cap Ferrat, which is renowned for its exclusive luxury homes. And like splashes of blue painted into the landscape, swimming pools of all different sizes glinted back at us in the late afternoon sunlight. Needless to say, Mum was very impressed, and putting the final touches to my shameless showing-off to her, we landed near my trailer. In the mornings, we played tourists, walking down to Casino Square to pick up an English newspaper, then having breakfast at the Café de Paris. One morning, I was flattered to see the local French paper, *Nice Matin*, had a colour photo of me and Jaka that had been taken at the previous night's performance slap bang on the front page! My mother was impressed.

The competition was split into two groups, with each separate group of acts taking its turn performing on alternate days. I managed to get tickets for Mother to see the first performance the dog act was scheduled to work in. Alas, she had never seen Prince work, and therefore couldn't draw a comparison to Jaka's performance; still, after the show when we got together in my trailer, she said how much she had enjoyed our performance.

Of course, her praise was very welcome, but I was also hoping for some criticism so that I could continue to improve the act. For some reason, however, that I can only put down to her not wanting to hurt my feelings, as my mother, she was vague and noncommittal. Also, although she didn't say so, it must have been strange for her to see the act again. I didn't feel like putting the question directly to her, but I wondered if it made her think of Dad and the old days.

On the last night, in company with most of the other artists, I waited outside a trailer where the jury was deliberating so we could hear the results of the competition first-hand. The jury that year was like a who's-who of show business and included Sean Connery and Cary Grant. Finally, at four in the morning, someone stepped out of the trailer with a list of winners. Hope had always been present, but as I expected, "Old Regnas" wasn't among them.

Prince had been like a gift given to me for just long enough to allow us to attain the necessary high standard that would get the act recognised in our niche of show business. The act with him made it possible for us to realise our potential and become a top attraction. We had come to people's attention and this acknowledgement carried through, even after his passing.

Mother left the day after the competition had finished, but I stayed on for another five days, during which I witnessed the dismantling of the tent and stables until nothing was left except the round outline of sawdust where the ring had been. On the last day of my stayover, even that was only just visible as the mistral, which had been getting stronger by the day, kicked up the last traces of those tiny dusty wooden particles that symbolise traditional circus and were lifted up and swirled away towards the open sea.

Not winning anything in Monte Carlo didn't bother me that much. We would have another crack at it, and I felt optimistic about the future, especially when I thought about how Kelly would turn out when trained. With newfound optimism, I left to do my second season with Barum.

*

I began to appreciate Jaka as a real trouper. Without him, I don't know what I would have done. He never faltered in his work, and for all his deadpan way of doing the act, he was always there, never ill, never missing a show. He was a real artist in the sense of "the show must go on". Jaka just kept going. If it was one show per day or even in some cases three, he didn't care – he always kept delivering.

Training a new dog was now routine for me, and I had Kelly ready to work during our third and last season with Barum, which was 1980. I encountered the same problem getting him used to the audience as I had with the other dogs, with the exception that he didn't run out of the ring and he didn't clam up like Jaka did. However, he lost his concentration and missed a few tricks.

Once a dog's actual training is done and I start to work him in the act, from there on it's best to give only minimal guidance and leave it up to the dog to develop at his own pace. Kelly quickly acquired a unique style which brought the act back up to the standard I was aiming for. In character, he was somewhere between Prince and Jaka, and although he was just a little slower than Prince, he was much livelier than Jaka. Kelly loved to work and his happy tail-wagging playfulness was in contrast to Jaka's somewhat expressionless, deadpan way of doing the act which, nevertheless, judging from the public's enthusiastic feedback, gave me the impression that they had been sufficiently entertained by what could fondly be called English dry humour (English *sheepdog* dry humour, that is).

Later that year, in an off-work period, Patchy got into a fight with another dog. Although the fight itself didn't seem to leave any outside sign of damage, later that same evening he became ill. I rushed him to the vet, where he was diagnosed with a stomach problem. I think the vet did everything he could to save him, but he died the next morning. An autopsy found an abscess on his liver. The abscess wasn't necessarily lethal, but the physical stress of the fight had ruptured it, causing internal bleeding.

Again I experienced the sadness of losing a dog. But I had chosen this life with them and as hard as it was to bear, I had to look for a replacement as soon as possible. There was just enough time to find another Jack Russell and train him to be ready for our next engagement, which was in Switzerland with the Knie Circus – the same circus where Dad had been working when he died, fourteen years earlier.

I found a new small dog and named him Chully. He was the toughest little dog I have ever encountered. It frightened me to learn that he was absolutely without fear and would stand up to the biggest dogs as though he were the same size. I always kept him on a lead when we went to work, because if we had to pass the lion's cage, he'd try and get to them for a fight. I think "Kamikaze" would have been a more befitting name for him.

Barny, Kelly, and Chully worked well together as a team. The act stabilised into its own category, alongside other popular circus acts, and we went from one engagement to another like Dad had done. We were successful. Not fantastic – not causing standing ovations – but we were good. The summer seasons, the winter seasons, Germany, Holland, Italy, Belgium, France, Austria – the engagements rolled on.

For me personally, the act took on a life and spirit of its own. Sure, there were the dogs, Barny and myself who made up the main part. But the act also consisted of the props, the music and the costumes to make it whole. I looked on the act as a living, breathing entity; everything included needed to be nurtured and fussed over. Sometimes, these sentiments took me to extremes.

I had a chair that I had used as a prop for many years. It was one of the few original items remaining from when I started the act. Over the years, other props were broken, what with all the moving about, and had to be discarded and replaced. The chair, however, seemed unbreakable and lasted a long time, and I became attached to it. When it finally broke, I couldn't bring myself to just throw it away in the rubbish. But I needed all available space and had to get rid of it. I decided I had only one choice.

One fine morning, with the broken chair in one hand and a spade in the other, I went looking for a decent spot to bury it. I found a field that seemed suitable, so I dug the hole, then lay the chair carefully and lovingly inside. Then I covered it with earth and stood for a few moments, solemnly contemplating all the places we had worked together.

*

Doing the act could sometimes be dangerous. One time we visited a town where we had to pitch the circus tent on a site that was very uneven. During the act, at the place when Kelly had to run and jump through my legs as I'm standing on my head, he stumbled in a dip in the surface of the ring just as he was taking off. Instead of passing through my legs, he crashed into my face with his front paws. I'd taken the lenses out of the glasses I wore at the time, but the wire rim broke and dug into the side of my eye. Blood streamed down as I did my best to finish the act without disturbing the audience too much. It must have looked like *The Rocky Horror Picture Show.*

Two other times I misjudged a trick with the cart and it hit me in the forehead, necessitating a trip to the hospital and stitches each time. Both times this occurred, it happened in a programme in which our act was slotted in between other much more dangerous acts, such as lions and tigers or trapeze acts that obviously presented a high risk to the performers. I had to laugh at the irony of it when I thought of them stepping out of the ring without a scratch, while I, with my relatively benign dog act, was exiting all bloodied. At the time, in a macabre way, I relished these events, as it gave me some distinctive recognition from those artists who were truly living life more dangerously.

*

Apart from Barny, of course, Jaka was now the granddaddy of the act. Although I used Kelly as the principal dog, I continued to use Jaka in the afternoon performances. As I gained experience working with the dogs, it was amusing to observe how each dog had his own style of executing his part in the act.

One of the things that stood Kelly apart and showed his professionalism was when, as part of the act, he'd take my hat in his mouth and run off with it, with me chasing him. In the beginning,

I trained him by throwing him the hat like you would play ball with a dog, so he learned to run around with the hat in his mouth. In time, though, it became a routine thing. Through patience on my part, he came to understand that it was part of the act, but he still did it because it was something he liked to do. Eventually, however, he also came to demonstrate how seriously he took his work: at the end of every act, as soon as he came out of the ring, he spat the hat out as quickly as possible. He knew the difference between work and play. That, to me, was an authentic show of professionalism.

In 1982, I contracted a virus that effectively put me out of work for most of the year. In no other business is the saying "out of sight, out of mind" more true than in show business, and I had a hard time finding work after my convalescence. In a way, it was again fate, because it caused me to look at all my options and branch out into other areas and venues for the act besides the circus.

After my recuperation, I received few offers for a while, and I was getting desperate when Billy Arata, one of the agents I always kept in contact with at the time, called me to say there was a dinner review show in Majorca who wished to copy Las Vegas shows that at the time were having a lot of success with animal acts on stage. The problem was, it was Friday and the proprietor had to have a video of the act on a VHS cassette on his desk by Monday. I was in the north of Holland and immediately took a train to Schiphol Amsterdam airport, where KLM had a special courier service for small packages that were given directly to the flight crew – since international terrorism has taken a hold, I doubt this service still exists. The very next day my video was delivered by KLM on arrival of their regular service to Palma and by Monday evening I received confirmation a contract for the coming season was on its way to me. "Es Foguero", in Palma De Majorca, turned out to be one of the nicest places I have ever worked. Our act was placed right after forty-five minutes of classical flamenco dancing by a very professional ballet ensemble. On the first night, I felt very out of place in a venue like that, coming up on stage following such a high-class artistic performance. To me it seemed quite a stretch to imagine that an old man, a donkey and two dogs could come out on stage and be considered funny after the audience had been put in the mood for classical entertainment. *No way is this going to work*, I thought.

I was completely wrong. We brought the house down and got nearly as much applause as the world-famous singing group The Platters, who were in the same show.

*

Since going out on my own to start the act, I'd kept in touch with my brother Peter. He was at Krone working as an assistant horse trainer. Alas, he was also finding it difficult to gain promotion and wanted a change. He had just as much right to Dad's act as I did, so I decided there would be enough room for both of us on the circus job circuit. Peter joined me at Es Foguero so we could train two dogs to get him started with his own act. We rescued the dogs from a pound and named the big one Copper. He was a mixed Dobermann; the smaller one, Dicky, was a Jack Russell mix. I knew Peter would face the same problems as I did when first starting out, but like me, he was glad to be more or less his own boss, and I was confident he would make it. We got the dogs trained and Peter set out on his own.

Because of the success of my act on stage, the next year found me in the same kind of theatre, this time on mainland Spain in the tourist town of Benidorm. The show was a new venture by some people who didn't have much show-business experience and, unfortunately, it was a flop. Business was so lousy that the show would have folded if everybody hadn't agreed to take a salary cut.

To add to those troubles, Jaka, who was now twelve years old, began to develop cataracts in both eyes. But his excited tail-wagging that began when I put my costume on convinced me to let him carry on working for as long as possible. It was amazing to observe that outside, he occasionally bumped into things, but performing the act was not really a problem for him. He'd been doing it for so long that he knew where everything was and when to do it. Also, I helped him by keeping my timing constant and always taking care to place the props in the same spot. Eventually, though, as the condition worsened, I had to stop working with him. Thankfully, apart from the eye problem he was fine and continued to stay fit. For his safety, I didn't let him run around free and kept him on a lead while exercising the other dogs.

The two summer seasons on stage had shown me that the act didn't have to rely solely on circus work. As long as the stage, or area, was big enough, it opened a whole lot of other possibilities for the future.

However, my stage career would have to wait a bit, because I had an offer to go to a circus in Italy.

*

Again my horse-training ability played a role in my popularity with the management of the new Italian circus, as I was able to help members of the family perfect their riding. I did this work for free, and they showed their appreciation by keeping me on for three years. The circus was modelled on the American system of three rings, and therefore called "Circo Americano". The first year, 1985, we toured in Italy and Sardinia. For the second year, the show ventured into France for the summer months, playing towns on the Riviera. It was like being on the Jean Richard circus again, with visits to the beach, coffee and croissants for breakfast – and, of course, finding a little spare time to work in the performances. I was having a good time.

One night, following an evening performance in the town of Le Grau du Roi, I decided to go for a ride on my bicycle. I wasn't sleepy and the dogs could wait a while for their last run before going to bed. The circus tent was pitched right in the middle of town in the tourist area. It was a cramped location where everything had to be squashed together as closely as possible. I recall that as I passed between some wagons and the stable tent, I had to duck my head underneath the guy ropes fixed to the tent, which stretched down to stakes driven through cracks in cobblestones.

Once on the open streets, I rode the short distance down to the harbour and the quaint cafés fronting the water on the quayside. It was quite late, but a few of the cafés were still open. With nothing particular in mind, I rode along, taking in the easy holiday-like atmosphere. From the cafés on one side of the street came the low sounds of taped music and people having a good time. On the other side, I could hear the soft clinking of rigging against the masts of yachts that rocked to a slight swell in the harbour. The sound reminded me of Chinese wind chimes.

"Hey, Mike," called a voice called from one of the cafés. "*Qu'est-ce que tu fais avec ton vélo, la? Viens boire un coup avec nous.*" What are you doing with your bike there? Come and join us for a drink." It was Robert from the circus office.

I acknowledged him, got off the bike, stood it against a wall and walked to the tables in front of the café.

"May I present Pascale? Pascale, this is Mike, the dog trainer."

I stared at this stunning girl with shoulder-length dark blonde hair and an hourglass figure sitting next to Robert.

"Pascale is our new head of ticket office duties," Robert said.

"*Bonjour, Mademoiselle,*" I said, taking her hand.

"You're the old man with the donkey and dogs?" she exclaimed. "I saw the show, and I would never have guessed."

"Yes, well, you see, I'm a young man."

We talked about circus life and, in particular, the animals. After a while I told them I needed to get back to the dogs and got up to leave. I did need to get back, but also, I thought Robert might be dating her and didn't want to intrude. Nonetheless, when I looked into the girl's blue eyes, I sensed something more than just her recognition of me as the old man in the dog act. It gave me hope that I'd made some kind of impression on her.

The next day, with all the confusion of a move to another town, I didn't have a chance to see Pascale, but she was on my mind. Then, the following morning in the turmoil of the build-up, I ran into her as she moved some things into the ticket office wagon. We both stumbled over our words in our efforts to make small talk. I told her that I'd tried to find her the previous evening because I wanted to invite her out for a meal.

"I was also looking for you," she said, averting her eyes for a second. My heart leapt! From that point on, for the rest of the summer, we saw a lot of each other.

Right at the beginning of our relationship, Pascale let me know she had a seven-year-old daughter named Mina. Before she had joined the circus, she and Mina had been living with Pascale's mother. Pascale had gone on to explain that Mina wasn't with her now, because she thought her job in the circus would only be short-term and leaving Mina at home with her mother to attend school was the best option.

A month after we first met, Pascale's mother, Janine, visited and brought Mina along with her. Mina was a beautiful child with long black hair and an olive skin tone that more resembled her grandmother's than Pascale's. Later, Pascale showed me a fashion magazine containing photographs of Mina modelling children's clothes.

Pascale didn't let on to Mina right away that we were seeing each other, but Mina quickly realised there was something going on between us. Even at that early age, she had a strong character and although she accepted me up to a point, I sensed she needed to feel she was still number one in her mother's life. I had to treat the situation with diplomacy. Even so, it was difficult in the beginning trying to make it clear it wasn't my intention to put myself between her and her mother. I knew things were getting better when one day she knocked on the door to my trailer and in one of those cute, quaint ways children sometimes have when they invent things, she asked if I had any eggs to cook so we could have a meal together. When I told Pascale later, she laughed and said, "That's strange, because she doesn't even like eggs."

Pascale's love for dogs was equal to mine, if not greater. In fact, sometimes I wondered whether her attraction to me wasn't more because of the dogs. Our romance in that first year together was an on-and-off affair. Up until then, I had always shied away from any deep relationship. But this time with Pascale it was different. Even though I believe we both felt we were serious about each other right from the beginning, I was still reluctant. I was thirty-nine years old and had always valued my freedom. During the times between my previous fleeting affairs, I still had the dogs to keep me company. "Who do I need?" had been my attitude.

But what if I gave in to my real feelings for her and accepted without reservation the togetherness I felt we both shared? Pascale wasn't from a circus family, and I wasn't sure she would take to the life full time.

My confusion and indecision had the effect of cooling our romance. We didn't really break off, but we saw less of each other. I'm not sure what Pascale's feelings were at that time, but she gave the impression she didn't want to waste time with someone stupid like me and assumed an air of aloofness whenever we met.

The summer season was drawing to a close, and we'd soon be going back to Italy. Pascale told me she'd be staying with Mina and her mother in France. One morning after seeing to the dogs, I went downtown to have breakfast at a café. I was just leaving when I nearly bumped into her coming in the door. We stopped for a moment, neither of us quite knowing what to say. I can't remember what we actually did say, but as I went to leave, she raised her hand

and carefully, lovingly, stroked a crumb off my cheek. The gesture was more intimate than a kiss.

Strangely, her touch on my cheek worked as though a magic spell had been placed on me, and it continued to haunt me for some time. And that wasn't the only thing. I kept thinking about our compatibility, her love for the dogs, her intelligence and, not least, her beauty. Unfortunately, I was too slow in putting my feelings and thoughts into action, and as the season drew to a close, she didn't change her plans to stay in France.

The following months, after Circo Americano arrived back in Italy, I couldn't get Pascale out of my mind. But we had no contact, because she hadn't even given me her address. The longer we were apart, the more I missed her. Experiencing that period without her snapped me out of my indecision and made me realise how much I loved and needed her.

I spent Christmas in Turin with the circus and then we had a month off, so I flew to England for a short break to see Ma and Mother. I arrived back to find that Pascale, together with Mina, had rejoined the show to take up duties in the office just before we all moved to Pisa. I was overjoyed.

The first days, we only saw each other occasionally in passing. I decided to invite her and Mina for a spaghetti dinner, so I bought a bottle of wine for the occasion and set everything up for a romantic evening. I cooked the spaghetti myself in the trailer. Luckily, the wine was good, because my effort at cooking wasn't. But Pascale didn't seem to mind and seemed glad to be there; happily, nothing could spoil our being together again. After the meal, Mina was tired, so Pascale took her back to the trailer the circus had provided and put her to bed. Then she rejoined me and although it was late, she persuaded me to go for a stroll.

We walked down to the old part of town. It was about 1am when we reached the open, floodlit area where the ancient monuments stood. The place was deserted and we stood alone on that cold January night in each other's arms, gazing at the beauty of the Leaning Tower of Pisa, with only the moon shining down on us for company.

The next day, Pascale and Mina moved into my trailer and we began to live together as a family. The circus provided a travelling school for the many children on the show, and Mina became a full-time pupil. Although Mina tolerated and even liked the dogs, she didn't share Pascale's deep feelings for them. But Pascale loved the dogs wholeheartedly and the dogs loved her. I discovered that as a child she had wanted a dog but was never allowed to have one because her mother didn't like animals of any sort. She could make up for that now.

*

Later that year, one of the circus dogs had a litter of puppies. The mother's name was Nancy and she was a mixed breed about the size of a poodle. With her long shaggy hair, she resembled a real mutt. During the time Nancy had been in heat, I had noticed all the male dogs of the circus community queuing up to mate with her – obviously that had been when the puppies had been conceived. At that time I had a strong suspicion that Chully had been among the dogs vying for fatherhood of Nancy's litter.

Nancy belonged to a Polish lady who would be going home after that season finished. Not wanting to be burdened with seven dogs, she desperately tried to find homes for the puppies before she left. That made me decide to take one of the males as an eventual replacement for Chully. I chose the liveliest one, and because we suspected Chully might be the father, we decided to call him "Attack", in recognition of Chully's bold character.

Two weeks later, homes had been found for all the other puppies except one female. She was the smallest and least developed of the bunch. One week went by, then another; nobody was interested in taking her. One morning, I saw Pascale approaching our living trailer, cradling a blanket in her arms. The little female dog was tucked inside. Pascale looked at me with a silent plea in her eyes, and when I peered at the bundle of fur in the blanket staring up at me, I couldn't resist Pascale. We decided to call her Mitzi. She would be the first dog we acquired who wasn't intended for the act.

After three years with Circus Americano, I was ready for a move. Pascale was also showing her gypsy spirit and was happy when I accepted an offer to go back to the Circus Barum in Germany. Barum also ran a travelling school, so Mina could continue to live with us.

In March, by the time we made the move to begin our summer season, Jaka had been in retirement for four years and was nearly sixteen years old. He was completely blind but still enjoying life. I had so much to thank him for. After Prince's sudden death, it was Jaka who carried the act through until Kelly was trained. He had remained the backbone of the act for many years. Now in his old age and despite his blindness, he was still quite active. I often spent time with him, just playing around. He enjoyed those sessions immensely, and we both rolled around on the floor together, finishing up with me laying him on his back and stroking his tummy. His head then lolled to one side and he would lie there completely relaxed. Through my ever-widening experience, I found that interacting with the dogs in an atmosphere of play was an indispensable part of our lives together. It kept them happy and mentally balanced. Not just with Jaka but with all the dogs, play made up a big part of our daily routine. It added to the general contentment with their lives, which showed in the happy way they did the act.

By the time we started work in Germany, Kelly was ten and had been doing the act for eight years. He was still going strong, and together with Chully, made a good team. There was no immediate need to find replacements for them; nevertheless, I thought now would be a good time to start looking for a new big dog because by the time he was trained, Kelly would be ready for retirement.

*

During the summer, we visited Baden-Baden, and Pascale found a dog-grooming salon in the paper so we could have Kelly looking his best for opening night. She became friendly with Claudia, the owner, and invited her to see that evening's performance. The next day, Pascale took one of the other dogs to be groomed.

"What a nice act you have, and the dogs really look as if they enjoy themselves," Claudia said. "I bet they have a good time living with you, otherwise, they wouldn't look so happy."

The conversation eventually got round to Pascale's mentioning that we were looking for a new dog. Through Claudia's work at the salon, she had contacts at the local animal shelter and told Pascale she'd seen a dog there that fit the description of the kind of dog we were looking for. She told us the manager of the shelter would be coming to see the show that evening, and we could speak to him about going to see the dog. After the evening performance, we were introduced to the gentleman and took him to our trailer to show him how the dogs lived with us. He was completely satisfied with the living conditions for the dogs and the way I looked after them and was more than pleased to fix up an appointment to see the dog that Claudia had in mind.

The next day we made an early start so we could be back in time for the afternoon show. But we weren't prepared for the reception we got at the animal shelter. After ringing a bell placed near a big wooden door at the entrance, we waited as the door was opened just a crack by a stout middle-aged lady. She held on to the edge of the door so as to block entry and asked us what we wanted.

When we introduced ourselves, she said, "No circus is taking any dogs out of here!" and slammed the door in our faces.

I was stung by the lady's outburst and somewhat bewildered by her prejudgment of us. The door was locked tight, so there wasn't much we could do but leave. I wanted to forget this unfortunate episode, but Pascale insisted on contacting the man we had met the previous evening to explain what had happened. She phoned Claudia with the information and Claudia said she'd get back to us. Later, she phoned to say the manager of the animal shelter was absolutely livid over how we had been received by the woman and said that if we were still interested in the dog, he'd meet us at the shelter at ten the next morning.

I was a bit reluctant, as I hate confrontations with ignorant people who think all animals in circus are ill-treated. But I decided to go, so the next morning we arrived on time at the animal shelter. We waited until the manager, Mr Seilbach, arrived a few minutes later. He told us how sorry he was about what happened.

"Those two women went too far this time; they think they run this place on their own and have nobody to answer to." He went on to explain that they had worked there for quite some time and didn't want *any* homes found for the dogs and cats in their care! They were always reluctant to let any of the animals go but previously hadn't gone so far as to bar entry to a would-be customer.

Mr Seilbach led the way towards the heavy wooden door and rang the bell. The same woman opened the door that had the day before, and when she saw him, she didn't say anything but stepped aside and let us in. I got the feeling that Mr Seilbach had phoned in advance, so they were prepared for this and reluctantly accepted the fact that their boss had the last say in the matter. The two women looked on sullenly as he led us into the back.

The manager went on ahead and opened one of the pens. Without any hesitation, a huge dog came bounding up to us, his tail wagging, and licked Pascale's hand. Keeping the act in mind, I always look for a happy dog and this one, in spite of being shut up in a cage, seemed very happy.

We learned his name was Wuschel. He was a really big dog, weighing about ninety pounds. He had medium-length, spiky, greyish-beige hair that stuck out at all angles. That's where he probably got his name, as the Germans say, *wuschelkopf*, meaning "mophead". Before we had left for the shelter that morning, I had told myself not to hold out much hope of finding a new dog that day and not to make any rash decisions. But from the moment I saw him, I knew "Wuschel" was a winner. He had an agility about him that is rare in such a big dog and seemed to move his weight around without any effort, as light on his feet as a ballet dancer. Also, his friendliness was captivating.

His papers said he was an "Afghan *mischling*", meaning "Afghan cross-breed". I found that doubtful; to me he looked more like an Irish Wolfhound crossed with a Briard. Just like the time we found Kelly, I thought that whoever had been responsible for filling out his paperwork had made a mistake. If the paperwork was done while the dog was still young and hadn't yet reached his adult looks, it would have been easy to do – especially if there was no way to verify what breeds the parents were, as is often the case with pound dogs. And sometimes whoever does the paperwork at the pound just puts down whatever seems to fit the dog's looks – it could make a mutt more appealing and adoptable if he has been elevated into a recognised breed.

I was a little apprehensive about how the two women would react when I said, "Yes, we want him," but no two ways about it, nothing was going to stand in our way of having Wuschel. I can't honestly remember what the two women said after they knew we were about to take him with us. As far as I can remember, it was kept to dark mutterings between themselves, probably because of Mr Seilbach's presence.

We paid the standard fee for taking a dog out of an animal shelter, which covered the cost of vaccinations, and put a hundred marks in a box with "donations" written on the side. When we got outside, something happened that seemed to be a bit of an omen, showing us that this dog was destined to be part of our family. As we walked out to the yard, Wuschel headed straight for our car, straining at the lead, and when we opened the door, he just dove in. How he knew it was ours I don't know.

So that's how we found "Bushel". Oh yes, of course – why "Bushel"? Well, Pascale couldn't pronounce "Wuschel" – or maybe, putting on her heavy French accent, she just pretended not to be able to manage the word – I'm not sure. (Pascale has developed her own methods of getting her way with me.) I thought Wuschel was quite a good name; but in the end, it got abbreviated to Bush.

The next day, Claudia filled us in on the dog's history, which surprisingly she knew quite a lot about. Apparently, a racehorse trainer had had his mother, but she had a litter of pups, including Bush, just at the moment he was preparing to emigrate to Australia. All the pups except Bush were destroyed, and when the man left, he just abandoned him and his mother at the racetrack. The story goes that his mother lived the life of a vagabond, getting food and shelter wherever she could, Bush trailing along with her. After about a year, someone new working at the racecourse enquired about the dogs and subsequently took them to the animal shelter.

To end this chapter, something happened that brought us a touch of sadness. A woman named Julia had already given Bush's mother a home before we found Bush. When Claudia came to visit us, she brought Julia and Bush's mother with her. To get a feel for the situation, you have to imagine us standing on this circus ground with all the living trailers parked parallel to a long road with a wall running along the whole length of the yard. The road wound off into the distance before disappearing round a corner; it was closed off to traffic and deserted. We met Julia with Bush's mother outside our trailer. Upon seeing his mother, Bush went crazy and made a general fuss over her. She, on the other hand, didn't act very interested in him and gave more the impression of wanting to be left alone.

We chatted for a while about all that had happened, and when it was time for them to leave, Claudia and Julia waved and walked down the road to their car, which was parked out of sight round the bend. As they walked down that long road, Bush strained and lunged against his lead, whining and trying to follow his mother. He made a big fuss, and I felt pretty rotten for having to restrain him. After a few moments he gave up and stood stock still, watching his mother go, an expression of sadness on his face that I'll never forget. If we can suppose that animals have thoughts and feelings similar to ours – and I firmly believe dogs do – then maybe flashes of memories of times with his mother were passing through Bush's mind. He continued to stand there and watch as she grew smaller and smaller in the distance, then finally disappeared around the curve in the road.

That profound look of sadness on his face affected us as well. It reminded me of some Charlie Chaplin film I once saw – Chaplin, with his genius, was able to make us laugh one minute and cry the next. Or perhaps it was a Disney film, in which situations were staged to play with our emotions and bring out our sentimental side. But this wasn't a film; it was real.

It's moments like this that make me understand better how to communicate with the dogs in their training. They have emotions like us, and it enables me to tune into those emotions and work as one with them, hopefully accepted by them as an equal.

*

As Attack lost his puppy features and began to transform into more of an adult-looking dog, it became obvious that Chully wasn't his father. He neither resembled him in looks nor character. But he was the right size to be the second dog in the act. "Attack" was much too aggressive a name for him, we thought, so we started to call him Tacki. He was a fast learner and in only a short time he was trained, making it possible to interchange him with Chully in the performances.

Later that year, Jaka developed an infection from a thorn in his paw. I'm sure it wouldn't have been life-threatening for a young dog, but his age was against him, and even with medication, it wouldn't heal. The infection spread through his body, and the veterinarian gave him little hope of recovery. He was suffering, so I made the heart-wrenching decision to have him put to sleep.

It wasn't like losing Prince, or even Patchy, because they were still fairly young when they died. I knew Jaka couldn't live forever, for sixteen years had passed since I took him out of that murky shed. Some of my sorrow was softened, knowing that his suffering was relatively short – only a few days earlier we'd been playing together. But Jaka was my first dog, and he would always remain special to me.

Bush was proving to be a real find – one in a million. The only slight problem I had to contend with was his obvious attachment to Pascale. He adored her and she adored him. I was caught in the middle and because I loved them both, I didn't know who to be more jealous of – him or her.

Well, all joking aside, I didn't mind, because not since Prince had I been so excited about a dog's potential for the act. He was alert, good-looking and, above all, he was keen to learn. During the training of all the other dogs, sometimes progress would take a step backwards. They would learn a trick to a point where I thought they were confident at performing it, then start teaching them the next trick. But occasionally I'd have to go back to retrain the previous trick, because small errors crept in. With Bush, it was different, he just went from one thing to the next. His capacity for learning the tricks was incredible. He almost preceded me in his knowledge of what came next, as if he were pre-programmed to learn the act.

Sometimes, my emotions over the dogs are exaggerated – but still, sometimes I wondered if Prince had come back to me.

*

That year, something occurred in the world of power and politics that I personally rank as one of the wonders of our time. We were playing in towns along the eastern border of West Germany when the television and radio news brought reports of East German refugees entering West Germany via Hungary. One of the towns we were visiting had a building that was used as a dispersal point for the refugees. The director of Circus Barum, Gerd Siemoneit, scheduled an extra performance with free admission just for them. At the time, his gesture mirrored the enormous goodwill of the West towards their east-of-the-border countrymen. Later, of course, the Berlin Wall was dismantled.

Pascale didn't share my amazed and joyful sentiments at the time, because she hadn't shared my experiences of years before when I'd been with Krone in West Berlin. At that time, we had to drive through the checkpoints at the transit corridors to get there and were subjected to intense scrutiny by armed guards. There were high towers on either side, manned by Russian troops with searchlights and machine guns. And if that wasn't enough to deter anyone from trying to escape to the West, there were sunken spikes in the road that could be sprung upwards at the touch of a button. Even when you had safely reached West Berlin, the daunting prospect of passing through Checkpoint Charlie remained, if you wanted to cross over to the East side.

At the time, I identified with the Germans and the euphoria and mass hysteria felt by all at the regained freedom. A newfound optimism was truly born. Still, I can't help but feel there was an opportunity missed there for forging new ground in understanding and cooperation. Over the next years, those initial joyful feelings of borders coming down and freedom of movement have proved much more complex, giving way to tensions and strife – mankind's business as usual. I count it a blessing that my gypsy way of life has enabled me to let go of my national or political identity to the extent that I identify with people of many different nationalities from widely varying cultures.

*

The year of 1989 brought important changes into our lives, as well. At the beginning of the year, Pascale and I got married.

We wanted Ma present for the ceremony, so we put the dogs into kennels for a few days and made the trip to England. We had just completed Christmas gala shows in France, and it was more convenient to leave from there because the short journey meant I could get back to the dogs as quickly as possible. A gala show, which was always good for filling in gaps in the budget, was a special, one-evening performance presented by a corporation or other group to an invited, often non-paying, audience. It was the first time I'd left the dogs with someone I didn't know well and could count on to act responsibly, and I was nervous for their wellbeing.

Now, as background, we had begun to change the act. I had only just started to realise the value of Pascale's contribution to our performance enterprise. She showed an aptitude for the business side of things, including talking to agents and negotiating the right price for an engagement. It freed my time and my mind to think about ways to make the act better. Pascale agreed with me that somehow, the act needed to be updated. The obvious and easiest way to start was with the costume. It had been over thirty years since Ma came up with her idea that Dad should be a tramp-like figure with baggy pants, with old-man makeup, etc. For fifteen years I'd donned the old man look. It had served as a shield between me and the audience and provided a way for me to deal with my

DAD *before he played the character of "Old Regnas"*

VICTORIA SANGER FREEMAN *1895 – 1991 my grandmother 'Ma' whose clever idea and choreography created the unique and original "Old Regnas" dog act*

"Lord" George Sanger 1827 - 1911 My second great grandfather

"LORD" GEORGE SANGER *1827 – 1911, my third great grandfather*

JAKA, *six months old, rescued from the shed*

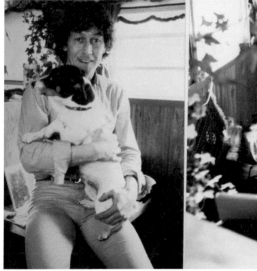

ABOVE:
TOP: *Altan, Theo, Patchy 2 , Tacki, Billy, Mitzi*
BOTTOM: *Out and In of 'Old Regnas' character holding my Jack Russell, Chully*

FACING PAGE:
TOP: *My father Pat Freeman - "Old Regnas" and Prince performing in front of a full house. Circus Knie Switzerland 1967*
MIDDLE: *Mike in the dressing room at the Circus Krone, Munich. ©Richard Baker 1984*
BOTTOM LEFT: *Mike in Old Regnas make up*
BOTTOM RIGHT: *The day I adopted Kelly at the dogs home in Bonn, Germany. The photo appeared together with an article in the national newspaper "Bild Zeitung" the next day*

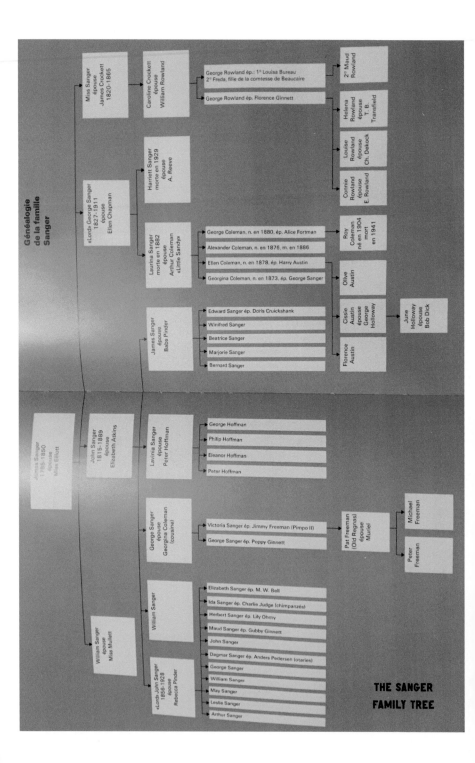

Généalogie de la famille Sanger

James Sanger 1785-1850 épouse Miss Elliott

William Sanger épouse Miss Mullett

John Sanger 1815-1889 épouse Elizabeth Atkins

Miss Sanger épouse James Crockett 1820-1865

«Lord» George Sanger 1827-1911 épouse Ellen Chapman

Caroline Crockett épouse William Rowland

George Rowland ép.: 1° Louisa Bureau
2° Freda, fille de la comtesse de Beaucaire

George Rowland ép. Florence Ginnett

2° Maud Rowland

Helena Rowland épouse T. B. Transfield

Louise Rowland épouse Ch. Dekock

Connie Rowland épouse E. Rowland

Harriett Sanger morte en 1929 épouse A. Reeve

Lavinia Sanger morte en 1882 épouse Arthur Coleman «Little Sandy»

George Coleman, n. en 1880, ép. Alice Fortman

Alexander Coleman, n. en 1876, m. en 1886

Ellen Coleman, n. en 1878, ép. Harry Austin

Georgina Coleman, n. en 1873, ép. George Sanger

Roy Coleman né en 1904 mort en 1941

Olive Austin

James Sanger épouse Babs Pinder

Edward Sanger ép. Doris Cruickshank

Winifred Sanger

Beatrice Sanger

Marjorie Sanger

Bernard Sanger

Cissie Austin épouse George Holloway

Florence Austin

June Holloway épouse Bob Dick

Lavinia Sanger épouse Peter Hoffman

George Hoffman

Philip Hoffman

Eleanor Hoffman

Peter Hoffman

George Sanger épouse Georgina Coleman (cousaine)

Victoria Sanger ép. Jimmy Freeman (Pimpo II)

George Sanger ép. Poppy Ginnett

Pat Freeman (Old Regnas) épouse Muriel

Michael Freeman

Peter Freeman

William Sanger

«Lord» John Sanger 1856-1928 épouse Rebecca Pinder

Elizabeth Sanger ép. M. W. Bell

Ida Sanger ép. Charlie Judge (chimpanzés)

Herbert Sanger ép. Lily Ohmy

Maud Sanger ép. Gubby Ginnett

John Sanger

Dagmar Sanger ép. Anders Pedersen (otaries)

George Sanger

William Sanger

May Sanger

Leslie Sanger

Arthur Sanger

THE SANGER FAMILY TREE

TOP: *Bush in action. Stadthalle Vienna 1991*

MIDDLE: *Performing as "Old Regnas" with Barny*

BOTTOM: *The early years of my horse career, riding the Lipizzaner Favory Betaika*

Festival du cirque à Monaco : deux cents artistes en piste

Le Festival international du cirque, qui, pour la cinquième année consécutive, se tient à Monaco, a débuté sous le grand chapiteau dressé sur l'esplanade de Fontvieille. 200 artistes (acrobates, clowns, dresseurs) parmi les meilleurs au monde vont se produire pendant cinq soirées pour l'émerveillement de tous et devant un jury qui compte dans ses rangs Cary Grant et Sean Connery. On voit ici Olé Regnas dans un numéro typique de comédie anglaise avec deux chiens.
(Photo René Briano).

ABOVE:
TOP: *Altan and Mike, Circus Scott, Sweden*
MIDDLE: *Pascale, Bush, Tacki and Mike, Friedrichstadtpalast Berlin*
BOTTOM: *Mike, Jaka and Kelly*

FACING PAGE:
TOP: *The hotel theme for the act. Studio photo taken in Copenhagen*
BOTTOM: *Press clipping on the front page of the 'Nice Matin' newspaper in 1978 "Festival du Cirque de Monte Carlo" with Jaka and Patchy.*

VIENNA STADTHALLE

press clipping photo

PASCALE

MIKE, **BUSH** *and* **TACKI** *Friedrichstadtpalast Berlin*

fear of audiences. So we decided to do away with that costume. At first it was difficult for me to do without the heavy makeup, the wig and moustache. I felt naked and awkward. But slowly I began to get used to it.

Up until then, the dogs had carried out all their tricks from the low pedestal that acted as a base for them throughout the act. Looking for more to improve things, I decided to make an addition to the routine in which Bush would hide inside a travel trunk at the beginning of the act, then continue to use that as a base instead of the pedestal. It meant making an extra prop and additional training for the dogs, but I thought it would be worthwhile for the extra comedy. The audience would be surprised when a dog jumped out of the trunk, did mischievous tricks and went back inside on his own without me supposedly having seen him.

Training Bush to stay in the trunk until a signal or cue was given for him to jump out was fairly straightforward and easy. However, to devise a way for him to go back inside on his own posed a technical problem. I found the solution by making the lid of the trunk wider than the vertical sides, so that it overhung the front by about two inches. This enabled Bush to get his nose under and lift it up. How did I train him to do that? Well, some things have to stay secret! Suffice it to say, there was no stress involved.

Back to our wedding. We arrived in London a day early, glad to find Ma in reasonably good health. She was nearly ninety but as clear in her mind as ever. At first I was apprehensive about telling her I was making changes to the act. After all, it had been her creation, and I wasn't sure she'd approve. But I finally got up the courage to tell her, and at first I thought her pensive look was a bad omen. I had so much respect for her that if Ma had been against any changes, I would have left the act as it was. But she didn't disappoint me. Her shrewdness and forward-looking attitude was as sharp as ever.

After a few moments' thought, she said, "I agree. Of course you have to move with the times, Michael. Let me know how things go."

I felt greatly relieved and fortified by her blessing.

The next morning, Mother also came up from Devon. Mina had been staying with her grandmother during our winter break, and they made the trip together with Pascale's sister and her three children. Despite having to use a cane, Ma insisted on walking the short distance to the City of Lambeth Registry office for the ceremony. Once we were seated in front of the magistrate, he began reading our vows. He must have mistaken Pascale's look of concentration for her possibly not hearing or understanding what he was saying.

The gentleman leaned forward to her. "You do understand what I am saying?" he asked in a low voice.

Even though I was in process of being married, it occurred to me that I could make a good comedy sketch out of this if I added, "Don't worry, I'll explain it to her later." But I resisted.

Pascale wanted to spend a few days in London with Ma, Mina and the rest of her family, but I was worried about the dogs, so I left immediately after the ceremony. The trip back alone gave me a moment to catch my breath after the hectic three days since leaving France. It also gave me time to reflect on my new status.

Previously, I'd been wary of being tied down to marriage. On the other hand, I was drawn by curiosity and often wondered what it must feel like to be married. At worst, I was afraid I might feel suffocated, and at best, it probably wouldn't make any difference at all. But afterwards I did feel different. It is hard to explain, but I just felt married, and I was happy. Above all, I knew I was lucky to have found someone like Pascale, who had all the qualities needed to share this crazy, nomadic life with the dogs.

When I got back to France, the dogs were fine, to my great relief.

While we had been on the road doing gala shows during the winter months, Mina had been staying at her grandmother's home so as to be able to attend regular school. It was obvious she was doing far better there than in the circus school. Although Pascale would have liked Mina to be with us always, in her view it was more important for her to have a good education, so with Mina's consent, it was arranged for her to stay on at her grandmother's to continue her schooling and visit us in her school holidays. It was a big sacrifice for Pascale, because she was torn between her life with me, trying to do the best for Mina and, of course, missing her.

Because of all the travelling involved, what to do about their children's education has always been a classic dilemma for show folk. Some of the big shows provide a school, but for performers in shows without that option, the choices are difficult. Some people think it best to stay together as a family and educate their children with the help of correspondence courses; others prefer to send them away, either to relatives or, for those who can afford it, to private boarding schools. Pascale's awareness of her responsibilities as a mother have always been very acute. Normally this is a good thing; however, it has given rise to a certain vulnerability in her that is at odds with her otherwise strong character.

The decision to send Mina away continued to play on Pascale's conscience to the extent that occasionally, when she reflected on her need to be with Mina, I could sense a deep feeling of sorrow. However, I believe Pascale has come to terms with her dilemma and realises that she is doing her best to make the right decisions for Mina and at the same time follow her destiny in our life together. At the risk of sounding selfish, I count my blessings that this situation didn't create a rift in our marriage.

*

When we returned to Barum in Germany for the summer, I concentrated on perfecting Bush's training to take the place of Kelly. I had visions of him becoming my second Prince and getting another shot at the festival competition in Monte Carlo.

With our changes to the act, I felt we might have a real chance at winning one of the coveted prizes there if Bush was able to meet my expectations.

The problem is, one doesn't just decide to do the Monte Carlo Festival. The acts that make it there must be of a high standard. And that alone doesn't even guarantee a place in the prestigious event. Politics also play a role. Because the festival is seen on television in so many different countries, the international flavour of the production has to be preserved. Balancing the selection of acts so they come from all over the world makes the selection pretty tight. Trusted agents send information about the acts they think are good enough directly to a selection committee. And the person to have the last word on which lucky acts are chosen to participate was none other than His Serene Highness, Prince Rainier. Although I had already begun to think and make plans in the eventuality of our being invited, it would have to remain something for the future. First, I had to be patient and finish Bush's training.

Many years had passed since I experienced the excitement of taking Prince to work in his first live performance. Jaka, God bless him, did everything, though without that extra bit of expressiveness needed to make the act star quality. It's only the dogs themselves who can supply the extra charm that reaches out to the audience, and it's the one thing I can't train into them. Either they have it or they don't. With his explosive energy, Prince had instantly catapulted the act to a higher level. After losing Prince to his heart problem, it was Kelly who took over the principal role alongside Chully and sometimes Tacki. Kelly had character and charm during the performance, and he was better than Jaka, but he was still a notch or two away from the impact Prince had had on an audience. Now, after eighteen months of training, it was time to try Bush in his first live performance, and the old excitement was back.

Three weeks previously, Bush had accomplished learning the final trick in the act. Since then, it had only been a question of rehearsing to solidify his performance and to make sure he was consistent. It was a hot day in late summer when I decided to try him out in a matinée show. We were in a small town in Bavaria and there weren't many spectators that afternoon. That suited me fine, because I didn't want the added pressure of working to a full house while concentrating on how Bush was doing.

Bush wasn't the only thing that would be new today. It would be the first time I tried out the improvements to the act, including having Bush hide in the trunk.

I made my entrance with Barny. After we did our funny bits together, I crossed my fingers and placed the first basket in front of the trunk. As I walked away to pick up the second basket, Bush jumped out of the trunk, pushed the basket over and dashed straight back to the trunk, lifted the lid with his nose and jumped inside. This was all done behind my back, which gave the impression to the audience that I knew nothing of what happened. I picked up the smaller of the baskets and because I was holding it in front of me, it appeared as if I couldn't see where I was going. As a result, I tripped over the basket that Bush had toppled.

I could tell that the new bit of having Bush hide in the trunk was making the act better. The audience loved the surprise of a dog coming out of the trunk and being so cheeky. But that wasn't all – Bush was fantastic! He wasn't disturbed in the least by the audience and he went on to work impeccably throughout the act. Extremely gratified at his performance, after the show I thanked him by stroking him and showering him with exclamations of "Good boy!" Bush had joined the ranks of true professionals.

*

I didn't realise how much Kelly loved working until I decided to retire him. He'd been doing the act the longest of any of the dogs. I thought it would make him happy to spend the rest of his life with me, just being a pet without having to do the act. Although Kelly wasn't quite up to Prince's standard for the act, that didn't mean that he was any less intelligent. His depth of character came through, as well as how seriously he took his work, when one night, instead of him, I took Bush for the evening performance. Kelly had become accustomed to Jaka working the afternoon performance and was okay with it when Bush stepped into that performance, but he knew the more important evening performance was allotted to him.

I'd been thinking of retiring Kelly for some time. He was eleven years old. Now that Bush was doing the act so well anyway, I didn't want to put unnecessary strain on Kelly.

Ma once told me a story from years ago about a dog named Bingo who had been part of an act on the Sanger show. Bingo was allowed to run free all day long. When the music for the act that performed before his act began to play, he'd turn up at the artist entrance, tail wagging and ready to perform. After his act, he'd come out of the ring and saunter off again to lead his own life.

I remembered this story as I went to take Bush instead of Kelly for the first time in an evening performance. From our trailer we could easily hear the band playing in the nearby tent. The juggling act music had just begun, which was our cue to get ready. Kelly knew the music and his ears pricked up in anticipation. At first both dogs looked surprised when I snapped the lead on Bush instead of Kelly, but when I attempted to leave, Kelly started to bark like crazy. I didn't want to shut him inside the trailer, so I tied him up with a lead. Although Pascale stayed behind to try to console him, he continued to bark loudly.

"Hey, it's me you should be taking," his barking words seemed to be saying, as he strained against the lead.

The next day when I took Bush for the afternoon act, which was normal, Kelly didn't react, but when it came to the evening show, he couldn't understand why I didn't take him and barked his protest.

This continued for another two days, with Kelly barking ferociously while Bush and I were in the ring. Then on the fourth day, something strange happened. This time, when I put the lead on Bush, Kelly surprised me. Instead of making a fuss, he just looked at me silently. He had the same sad expression as the first day we saw him, when I passed him by at the dog pound. At that moment, I sensed he finally understood the inevitable – that Bush had taken over.

For the next few days, as I continued to take Bush instead of Kelly, Kelly's sadness added a sombre mood to our preparation for the performance. To help Kelly adjust, Pascale started taking him shopping with her and on any other short journey she had to make in the car. He had always liked travelling, and when Pascale called him and opened the door of the car, his tail started wagging as he jumped inside, and he wouldn't budge until he'd been somewhere and come back again.

Shortly after Bush became the principal dog, we received a call from my friend and agent, Roberto Germains, to ask if we would like to go to the Scott Circus in Sweden the next year. We could have stayed another season with Barum, but I was excited about the prospect of going back to Sweden and hopefully visiting some of the places in which Dad had worked. The decision to go was unanimous – Pascale was getting itchy feet again – so I asked Roberto to send the contract as soon as possible.

For the past two winters, we'd been doing gala performances in France, mostly on stage in small theatres. Pascale's sister had a home in Normandy, so when we had time off between jobs, we stayed at her place. It was within easy reach of the rest of Europe and made a convenient base for us. In March 1990, we set off from Normandy to join the Scott Circus in Sweden.

The overnight trip by boat from Travemunde in the north of Germany to Trelleborg, Sweden, was very pleasant, but on arrival, we faced a lot of hassle concerning the dogs. Only working dogs were allowed entry into Sweden without having to go through the rigours of quarantine, so our papers were scrutinised for appropriate shots and proof that they really were working dogs. Finally, we got those formalities behind us and made the short trip to Malmö, where the circus was located.

*

I have always liked the Scandinavian countries and felt immediately at home in Sweden with the Scott show. The act in its premiere performance was an immediate success. The next day, Pascale and I were walking downtown and passed a newsstand. There, on the front page of the local paper, was a big photo of Bush. The picture was magnificent. The photographer had captured him in all his glory, suspended in mid-air about four feet off the ground as he passed in between my legs while I stood on my head. Bush's ears were flat against his head and his spiky, light, beige-coloured hair was flying in all directions, all against a black background. The photo stood out because it was the only one in full colour. We immediately bought five copies.

Mr Bronnett, the boss of Circus Scott, was one of the nicest people I have ever worked for. He had a certain eccentric class that stood him apart from most other circus directors. He was a revered figure, not only in the circus world but as a public icon, and known all over Sweden. Mr Bronnett's eccentricity manifested itself in subtle ways. To complement his persona as a circus proprietor, he also played the role of ringmaster, announcing the acts. On payday, one of his little quirks was to sometimes enter the ring when an artist was in the middle of his act and present him with his pay cheque. A juggler of top hats found his pay cheque in one of them. Another time, a performer was offered his cheque in an ornate envelope, placed on a silver platter and presented to him in the middle of the ring just as a drum roll was building the suspense for his big trick.

We also discovered Mr Bronnett was on the organising committee of the festival in Monte Carlo. The huge success the dog act enjoyed in every performance hadn't escaped his attention, and he volunteered to propose us to the selection committee to our great delight. We heard nothing more about it for some time. Then, one evening during the show, just as Barny and I had just arrived at the place where I pushed and shoved him in an effort to make him move forward, I felt an added presence in the ring. I looked up. Mr Bronnett was standing on the other side of Barny with a big grin on his face. He put his left hand over the microphone and leaned over Barny's back to get closer to me. With the music playing I could barely hear him.

"I spoke to the Prince today – it's okay, they want you for the Monte Carlo Festival." He took me completely by surprise, and I froze. All I could manage was to dazedly nod my head up and down. Mr Bronnett certainly had a flair for the dramatic, and he really "got" me that time. Later in our trailer, Pascale and I talked over the upcoming festival and made our plans, excited at the wonderful opportunity.

After we finished our season with the Scott Circus, we returned to France, where we did our usual gala work. Then, just as we began preparing for the Monte Carlo Festival du Cirque, full of optimism, the Gulf War started. A foreboding atmosphere fell over France – people were very uneasy, and many rushed to the supermarkets to stock up on food. There were long lines at the petrol stations. Stories began to emerge about how badly business was being affected – especially the tourist-dependent shows in Paris, like the Lido and the Moulin Rouge. The fear of terrorist attacks in public places drove people away. Then came the inevitable news – the sixteenth Monte Carlo circus festival had been cancelled.

Pascale and I were very disappointed at losing our hard-won chance. The cancellation also posed a work problem for us, because we had nothing else lined up for the summer. We were hoping a success at the festival would get us scooped up by some top show. It was February, and we had to find something soon, before everybody had their programmes fully booked up.

After some phoning around, we had a chance meeting with Conny Gasser, the owner of Connyland, a well-known amusement park in Switzerland. He needed an act like ours for the summer season, so he engaged us to work on stage in the vaudeville theatre, which was one of the park's main attractions. During our stay there, I continued working to improve the act. We replaced the baskets with custom-made leather cases and had new music specially composed and recorded to accompany the act. All in all, it was looking really good. One last item – because of the modifications, the act began to conform to my own style, so I thought a name change was in order. I decided to revert "Regnas" back to "Sanger", and call the act simply, "Mike Sanger".

4

I ALWAYS KEPT IN TOUCH WITH MA. We wrote letters to each other, and I phoned her often. She lived on her own after Sissy, her flatmate, died. Apart from minor health problems over the years, she was fine. Once she had to go into the hospital for cataract surgery, but the operation went well.

On a short trip to England in May 1991, I had a very enjoyable visit with Ma. She was still walking with her cane, but otherwise she seemed in good health. Not long afterwards, after I had returned home, I received a letter from her saying she had to go into St Thomas's hospital, one of the best in London, for some routine tests. I phoned the hospital and managed to get through to her room and spoke to her. We had a short conversation and she sounded okay. I remember she told me not to worry.

That was to be the last coherent conversation I had with her. The next day I had a call from Mother to say that Ma had suffered a stroke while still in the hospital. I took the first available flight from Zurich to London next morning, leaving Pascale to look after the dogs and Barny. I'd arranged to meet Mother at the entrance to the hospital, and we both went up to the top floor where the geriatric ward was located. After checking with the sister in charge, we were led to Ma's bed. The nurses were making her bed, and she was sitting in a wheelchair, staring straight ahead. I knelt in front of her.

I had never felt uncomfortable with my grandmother; we understood each other and conversation had always been easy. But this time I didn't know what to expect. "Hello, Ma," I said, a bit hesitant.

She looked at me, and I noticed how her mouth slanted to one side.

In a slurred voice she said my name. "M-i-chael." She continued in that painfully slow, slurred tone, that seemed so strange to me. "I haven't seen you for a long time."

"No, Ma," I said.

Mother pulled up a chair, and Ma recognised her and called her by name.

"How are you, Ma?"

"I feel so tired."

This exchange made me hopeful that she had escaped serious brain damage and that it was only a question of time for her to get better. But then she drifted away and began to talk to us as if we were strangers. It was painful to see her in that state, not really knowing who we were.

We were allowed to take Ma outside, and I pushed her round the hospital grounds for a while in her wheelchair. It was a warm, sunny day, and we stopped at a cafeteria with chairs outside. I bought some ice cream. Ma couldn't lift her arms, so Mother played nurse and helped her eat her portion. Later, when we arrived back at the ward, I kissed Ma on her forehead and said goodbye. I had to get back, but Mother said she'd stay with a friend in London for a few more days, so she could continue to visit with Ma.

In our business, bosses are notorious for not being very happy when an act is missing from a show. I was lucky this time to have an understanding one. There are some who wouldn't have let me go, even for this short time. I remember an occasion several years earlier when a member of an act had passed away. The other members of the family who were also part of the act went to bury the person two hundred miles away in their hometown and had to miss one afternoon performance. When they returned from the funeral, the owner of their circus made his disapproval very clear indeed. His motto, "The show must go on," was a harsh reminder of the often false glamour of circus life.

For a few days there was no change in Ma's condition, but then I received a call direct from the hospital to say that she had worsened, and if I wanted to see her one more time I needed to come within the next few days. Again, my employers let me go. This time I was on my own when I arrived at the hospital. Ma was no longer in the main ward, and I was shown into a private room. When I saw her, I was shocked by her appearance. With sunken features, she no longer resembled the person I knew – certainly not the beauty of old family photos, the clever choreographer of the act, or even the regal, mature woman of later years.

I stood for a while at her bedside. Her eyes were closed and I don't think she knew I was there. Now and again she turned and twisted, like someone having a bad dream. I turned to look out of the window at the splendid view of the Houses of Parliament and Big Ben across the River Thames. Although she had travelled most of her life, Ma had the right to call herself a Londoner – a real Cockney – because, as tradition would have it, she was born within earshot of Bow Bells.

Although it was hard to accept, I knew Ma was dying. It was ironic and appropriate, though, that after a lifetime of travel and uncertain destinies, her life would end here in the heart of London. Strangely, just outside the hospital is the site where the original Astley's Amphitheatre once stood. Astley's was the first circus of modern times and was described by Dickens in his novel *The Old Curiosity Shop*. Ma's great-grandfather, "Lord" George Sanger, was the last circus proprietor of Astley's before he was forced by the City of London to close it — after which it was demolished. The garden of St Thomas's Hospital where we had eaten our ice cream a few days earlier now occupies the spot, and the Amphitheatre is commemorated there by a memorial stone.

I came again to the bedside and clutched Ma's shrivelled hand in mine. I wanted to imprint this moment into my memory, when I said my last goodbye to her.

Six days later I got a call from the hospital to tell me that Ma had died. She was ninety-six. The following week, an obituary appeared in the *Daily Telegraph* titled "Death of an Elephant Queen". Accompanying the obituary was a black and white photo of an oil painting of Ma in Indian Rajah costume, done by Lucy Kemp-Welch, a well-known equestrian painter of the time who had travelled with the Sanger show. The article was one column wide and ran down half a page. I was proud and thankful for this not-insignificant tribute to the remarkable woman who had been my grandmother and in no small way, my professional mentor.

*

Later that year we travelled from Switzerland to France, then on to Milan for a Christmas show. The winter of 1991 was a busy one for us but kept us in training for the big Monte Carlo festival in February. When the previous year's event was cancelled because of the Gulf War, we were one of the lucky acts to have had our contract renewed for the next one.

The setting for the festival had changed enormously since I had last performed there in 1978. At that time it had been held in the "Egnis Togni" Circo Americano circus tent, pitched on an enormous piece of what appeared to be wasteland but was in fact land that had been reclaimed from the sea. I think the land was in the process of being allowed to settle before it could be built on.

The tent, together with the adjoining stables, had all looked very makeshift and forlorn in that open space, and stood in stark contrast to the rest of elegant Monte Carlo, visible in the background. The Palace, positioned especially high, appeared to be standing guard over the circus Big Top.

Now it was completely different. The landfill had been rendered unrecognisable by posh apartments, a magnificent hotel and other new buildings that had sprung up to make a whole new community. In the midst of this modern addition to the Principality there were quaint little patches of green landscaped to perfection, with paths running through them and park benches placed here and there. Continuing on towards the sea, we arrived at the picturesque building – le Chapiteau de Fontvieille – where the festival was to take place.

The circus building resembled a typical, round European circus tent; however, while the roof was made of tent material, the sides were solid walls. This meant the structure remained standing each year, a permanent fixture able to withstand the strong mistral wind that plagued the region each year. The interior followed the lines of all modern circus tents, with a notable feature being the absence of poles. In the older tents, these obstructed part of the audience's view. As a reminder that performances would be graced by the presence of His Serene Highness Prince Rainier and the rest of the royal family, the interior was decorated with plush seating and carpets that made it more resemble the interior of a theatre than a circus tent.

Pascale and I were directed to put our truck and trailer near the artists' entrance. The competing acts had been flown in from all over the world and most were lodged in hotels. For convenience, animal acts, each with their respective transport, had places reserved for them near the tent structure. Our designated area was between a horse stable and a tent that housed two elephants.

The competition was scheduled to run for five days, with three days prior to that allotted for rehearsals. Twice as many acts would participate in the competition as could be accommodated in one performance, so the performers were split into two groups. Each group presented its acts in separate performances that occurred on alternate days.

Mina wanted to be with us for the festival. She had become quite an independent young lady by now, so she made the trip to Monte Carlo alone by train.

When we started rehearsals, it was evident the competition would be fierce, with big attractions from North Korea, China and Russia comprising troupes of five to ten people each. Those countries had state-run circuses and special state-run schools to supply a steady stream of talented artists who were trained to a very high standard. The acts formed in those schools were put together by professional choreographers, and their music was arranged by experts at no expense to them. One of the Chinese acts involved artists swinging around on bungee cords and was particularly impressive. It was accompanied by haunting music, which gave the act that bit of extra magic.

Also, there was a flying trapeze troupe from North Korea whose mainstay was daring somersaults. Standing on his perch, the star flyer of the act acknowledged a signal from the catcher sitting on his "cradle" some thirty feet away on the other side of the tent. He launched himself on the trapeze bar and swung down, then up again. On the second swing down, he positioned his body, arms straight out, head level with the bar and toes pointed. Now he was fully committed to the most difficult trick of all. At the top of the swing, he flung himself away and upwards from the trapeze bar, immediately curling his body into a tight ball, which made him turn at unbelievable speed. One, two, three turns, then, with split-second timing, he flipped his body straight and his hands stretched out to find those of the catcher.

Clap!

That sound and the little puff of powdered magnesium as the hands slapped tight in each other's grip signified the successful completion of the trick. The crowd of hushed onlookers released a sigh of relief.

These were the acts in contention for the big prizes – the Gold Clown and the Silver Clowns, which were the Oscars of the circus world. After the Clowns came the special prizes, awarded by different sponsors, companies and societies. One of the most significant or prestigious special prizes was probably the SBM (*Société des Bains de Mer*). It was awarded to the act thought most deserving by the society comprising the founding fathers of the resort of Monte Carlo. Those members are also the owners of the world-famous Casino. The SBM, with its relative freedom from political influence associated with the jury prizes such as the "Clowns", is one of the most important prizes. The last time I came to the festival, I knew we didn't stand much chance of winning anything, but this time my hopes were higher. Barny was a seasoned pro and Bush and Tacki were in their prime, so I could rely on everybody to give their best. Also, our choice of music from the Federico Fellini film 8½, which had been arranged to synchronise with and fit the character of the act, gave me added confidence. This time there would be no playing the tourist, strolling down to Casino Square and having breakfast at the Café de Paris while leisurely reading my English newspaper. There was no time for that. This time I had to stay focused – nothing would be left to chance.

I practised the act every morning and in the afternoon I worked on the props – a touch of paint here, a loose screw tightened there – to make sure everything would function and look its best. Pascale volunteered to help me groom the animals. Barny's coat shone, and a dressing of neat's foot oil on his tiny hooves made them look like polished boots. Small details, but everything counted. This time I was determined that we would go all out and win something.

The first day of competition was looming. My growing nervousness at performing in front of such a prominent audience reminded me that I was probably the weak link in our presentation of the act.

"I must stay calm," I kept telling myself. However, there was a positive side to my nervousness, because I also felt great excitement at showing off the act and letting everybody know how good we were.

On the first day of the competition, Mr Bronnett from Circus Scott came to wish me good luck. Later that evening, as I waited behind the curtain for our call, I tried to switch the feelings from self-doubt to concentration on doing a good act. I owed it to the dogs and to Barny. I felt confident that my training had done its part and they were at their peak. Now I mustn't let them down by feeling intimidated by the audience and not giving my best.

Our music started to play and when the curtain opened I flapped the reins over Barny's back to cue him to move forward.

"Gee up, Barny," I called, as we made our entrance. Trying not to feel nervous was easier said than done, and I was very conscious of the Royal Box just the other side of the ring fence. At first, the audience was a bit cool. They were a seasoned crowd of spectators, the same ones coming back year after year, and very discerning and critical. You could hear them thinking, "Show us what you can do before we show our appreciation." They were, in effect, a professional audience.

As the act progressed the crowd warmed to us, and finally when I took my bow, the applause left no doubt of our success. I remembered the time Dad had performed in front of Princess Margaret. The audience was a snotty-nosed lot who either didn't want or were too afraid to laugh or clap.

But because the Monte Carlo audiences were used to seeing only high-quality acts, I believe they weren't snobbish, just discerning.

The next day it was the other groups' turn for their performances, and the day after that it was our turn again. (Everyone had two chances to show their acts to the jury.) We did a bit better the next time, mainly because I was less nervous, which enabled me to express my role better.

Even so, in fear of disappointment, and also not wanting to give any false hopes to Pascale, I hesitated to rate our chances of winning anything. I thought the act had been a success, but then many of the others had also been successful. But, I thought, we had done our best – now it was up to the voting and we would just have to wait and see.

Awakening the next day, I felt lighter, no longer feeling the stress of participating in the competition, with its demand on us to constantly do our best. To help me unwind from the week's events, I took the dogs for a long walk, then spent the rest of the afternoon with Pascale in our trailer, where we contemplated our chances.

That evening everybody was invited to Loews' Hotel for the awards dinner banquet, where the winners would be announced. The reception was lavish, with many celebrities present. Pascale looked ravishing in a new dress she had bought for the occasion, and Mina looked cute in a black skirt and white blouse. I could tell she was impressed by being up close to so many celebrities.

As we sat at our table, my mood vacillated from quiet resignation to expectant hope. We had done our best and from now on I was out to enjoy myself. But no matter the outcome of the competition, I felt proud of us as a threesome and of our success. However, Pascale's mood was a little different. I felt sure nothing short of being among the winners would keep her from feeling depressed.

Later in the evening, after the wining and dining was over, the moment arrived that everyone had been waiting for. An official from the organising committee was handed a microphone. After a short speech to gain everybody's attention, he started to announce the winners.

A cleverly choreographed contortionist act involving four young girls from Cirque du Soleil, together with the North Korean and Chinese troupes, won the Gold and Silver Clowns. After the applause for those nominations died down, the official began to announce the Special Prize winners.

"*Le Prix PAVDEC*" – *Prix de la Presse Associée des Variétés et du Cirque* – "Mike Sanger!" he called into the microphone.

But I hardly had time to realise that we had won one of the more prestigious special prizes before once again, I heard my name.

"*Le Prix, SBM*" – the coveted "*Société des Bains de Mer*"! – "Mike Sanger!"

Two prizes, and one of them was the SBM! I couldn't believe our luck. I was immediately congratulated by two circus directors who were sharing the table with us – the first was Mr David Smart, who had booked me for the Eurovision TV show in 1975, and his family from England. (Their daughter Yasmine had also taken part in the festival.) The second was Mr Tihany from the Tihany Circus in South America.

This was a moment to hold on to, and a deep feeling of pride engulfed me. Mina was ecstatic and Pascale leaned across the table to reward me with a kiss on my cheek. But our success had been a team effort and I was equally indebted to Pascale for her support, and of course, the dogs and Barny, who had all risen to the occasion and given their best performance.

Later, after I had taken the dogs for a walk and before turning in for the night, I squatted down on the floor with Bush and Tacki.

"Thanks, boys," I said, running my hand through Bush's thick spiky fur and ruffling Tacki's ears. I spent a few minutes longer with them than usual, then I went to bed. Lying there in the darkness, I thought about the gala performance tomorrow, when all the winning acts would put on one final show – after which the prizes would be presented. I felt like a kid excited about waking up to his presents on Christmas morning, and sleep didn't come easily.

The next morning we were handed a business card by a secretary for the agent who booked acts for the Lido in Paris (the most famous nightclub in the world). A note was attached, asking us to telephone her. Later, my agent, Roberto Germains, phoned to say that a film company was interested in my services as a dog trainer. And another agent, who booked mostly for cabaret, asked if it was possible to do the act without Barny.

Things were happening so fast! *It's amazing what winning something at Monte Carlo can do for business*, I thought.

During the gala performance next evening, I felt more relaxed and less intimidated by the audience. As a result, the act enjoyed even more of a success than in the competition. But I still felt a momentary annoyance at my lack of professionalism. *You must not let uneasiness in front of audiences affect the performance of the act*, I reprimanded myself.

As soon as the performances ended, the artists were invited to stand in the ring towards the back, and one by one, they called the winners to the centre to receive their prizes. I was called in twice. The bronze statues which represented the PAVDEC and SBM prizes were by Kees Verkade, a celebrated sculptor whose works demand high prices, and were presented to me by Prince de Polignac of Monaco, Prince Rainier's uncle.

Standing in the ring on that grand occasion, I thought of Ma and Dad and wished they could have been here and feel their pride at all my hard work and now, my hard-won success in carrying on the good name of Sanger and the legacy of the Old Regnas act.

*

Mina had taken leave from school just for this special occasion. Soon she would be taking her pre-university baccalauréat exams and she didn't want to miss out on her studies, so she left straight after the competition finished. Although we were apart most of the time, my bond to Mina had grown stronger over the years and I was glad this short interlude had been a happy time for her.

We considered our options for work, and although places like the Lido had shown interest in us, the engagements weren't for the immediate future, so we decided to pursue the offer from the film company. The pay would certainly be more than we could ever earn with the dog act. Also, the challenge of doing something different interested me; maybe I could make a name for myself in the movie business as a trainer, I thought. I didn't want to stop doing the act, but now and again some film work would help us financially.

The high salaries I had been able to command when I started out with the act were now hard to come by, what with many of the circuses filling their programmes with relatively cheap but high-quality acts from Eastern-bloc countries. Since the fall of communism, all those well-trained artists from the special schools could come and go as they pleased, so now the market was flooded with good acts. In the past, those acts had remained exclusive to the big shows that had the political clout necessary to bring them over to the West. Now, one could visit any small circus in Europe and find the performances enriched with acts from Russia, Bulgaria, Romania and other countries that had once been part of the Soviet Union.

I met with the movie people in Paris and was handed the script for the film they wanted to make. Upon reading the script, I found that my work would entail training two dogs various tricks, among them playing Frisbee and changing channels with a TV remote. According to the script, the dogs would be central to the story, and there would be a lot of work involved. Further negotiations seemed to be going to plan, but then I didn't hear from them for some time. Finally I was informed that the whole project was put on hold. It was March and too late for us to find a long season engagement – all the shows had their programmes fully booked by then. So what promised to be an exciting year for us turned into a dilemma. We were full of high expectations after winning the prizes in Monte Carlo but had now been left high and dry for work. For most of the summer, we found ourselves sitting at home in Normandy, waiting by the phone for the occasional offer. It was a hard time; however, partly due to those circumstances, a big change would soon come about in the way we presented the act.

It started with a phone call one day in late August from an agent we knew.

"Mike, are you free to do a TV show in Italy three days from now?"

"That's impossible," I said. "I need at least a week to get the paperwork done to get my donkey into Italy." (My smuggling days were over.) But since we were desperate for work, I asked him to hold the line while I took a moment to collect my thoughts. A few weeks earlier I'd had an idea to get Pascale into the act. Instead of Barny leading the way onto the stage, it would be Pascale, playing the elegant lady traveller, and I'd be taking care of her luggage. I put the phone to my ear again. "Listen, I have an idea for Pascale to take the place of Barny."

I heard laughter on the other end of the phone.

"In that case, we just have to travel with the dogs, so it won't be a problem to get over the border."

"Okay, Mike," said the agent, still chuckling into the phone. "I trust you to give a good performance. Do whatever you feel is necessary, just get there on time."

I explained to Pascale my idea, and she enthusiastically accepted the idea of playing a role in the act. That evening, I set about making a handcart to take the place of Barny's cart. It was composed of two handles sticking up from a platform made with a five by two foot piece of plywood. Underneath that I fixed an axle and two wheels I scavenged off an old wheelchair. It looked a bit makeshift, but with a new piece of blue carpet covering the flat bed and some paint on the handles and wheels, it would have to do.

Pascale's part would be to set the theme for the act with a plausible beginning. The next day we had just enough time to rehearse a short, sketch-like routine before it was time to get on the road to the city of Rimini on the Adriatic coast.

It was strange to be on our way to an engagement without Barny. We left him in the capable hands of a friend who made his living training jumping horses. He promised to let Barny out to pasture in the daytime and at night take him into the stable barn, where a huge box normally used for horses was prepared for him with plenty of bedding straw and hay to eat.

After a day and night of travel, it was late morning when we arrived at our destination. The stage and auditorium were outdoors. We did a run-through of the act so the television cameras could get the right angle shots. Afterwards, we still had plenty of time before the show, so we grabbed something to eat, then rehearsed the routine that would replace the part with Barny.

The idea was for Pascale to make her entrance onto the stage with Tacki on a lead. I followed her, pushing the small handcart with the luggage on top. I placed the cart in the middle of the stage and doffed my hat to Pascale. She pretended to give me a tip, then she left the scene and I carried on with the normal routine of stacking the luggage. It was simple, but with such limited time to prepare ourselves, it was safer than trying to do something complicated.

The performance would be transmitted live and was a typical Italian Saturday-night spectacular set in a hot vacation nightspot, mixing variety acts with a quiz show as the main theme. The acts were supported by a dance ensemble of long-legged beauties. To add to this chaotic scenario, the variety acts would be competing against each other, something like a television game show, except there were no prizes.

We still had three hours to kill before the show started, so we drove to our hotel for a shower and some rest. We had only Bush and Tacki with us for this trip, having left the other dogs back in France with Pascale's sister.

Feeling refreshed, we returned to ready ourselves for the performance. Knowing that the programme would be transmitted live and we were trying something new made me somewhat nervous. Pascale must have been even more nervous than I was, but she didn't show it. Bush and Tacki were probably wondering where Barny was.

For about an hour the public had been arriving and the place was beginning to fill up. Music was playing and people danced on the stage, creating a party atmosphere even before the show began. After the stifling heat of the day, the balmy evening breeze that ruffled through my shirt was both soothing and invigorating. The cooler temperature also had a good effect on the dogs. They were livelier and after a long layoff were eager to do the act again.

The variety acts were slotted in between dance routines and short interludes in which contestants answered questions in the quiz part of the show. But it was all good fun and most of the questions were presented in a way that would get a laugh, rather than being difficult to answer.

Ours was the last of the variety acts scheduled to perform. The compere – the host – of the show continually encouraged the audience to make as much noise as possible for their favourite act, so a decibel machine could register the highest marks to determine a winner. The quality of the acts that night wasn't as high a calibre as most of the acts at Monte Carlo; even so, I had no idea how the public would react to us, especially in our new version without Barny.

I was surprised when the audience members were so enthusiastic about our act that we won the competition. The most significant result of that evening, however, was how Pascale and I sensed this could be a new way to do the act, making it just right for cabaret and stage. When Dad started out, the Old Regnas character he and Ma created was right for the times. Now, perhaps it was time to move on. This would be a novel way to modernise the act and enable us to work in venues otherwise inaccessible to us. Sometimes lack of space prevented Barny from working, but also, in some places, the character of the act didn't fit because they didn't want acts which were too circuslike. With this one simple manoeuvre, the act had taken on a new identity and a more plausible meaning for a modern public. The real success of that evening was how well Pascale played her small but significant part, and I was really proud of her.

*

That winter, we were scheduled to fulfil an engagement in Berlin at the Friedrichstadtpalast, self-billed as Europe's largest revue show theatre, in what used to be East Berlin. The contract had been signed before we did the Italian TV show, so the show was supposed to be with Barny. I was anxious to give the act with Pascale a chance and felt it was much better suited for the theatre. I should have asked the bosses of the theatre if I could leave Barny out of the act and instead do the sketch-like routine with Pascale, but I was afraid they would insist I honour the contract as it stood.

When we arrived for the engagement, I explained that Barny would be arriving a week later and in the meantime I would do the act with Pascale. The bosses of the theatre were not happy, because they wanted the same act they had seen on the videotape that had been sent by the agency. My tactic nearly got us fired, but I was confident that when they saw the act in its new form, they would agree to keep it as it was. So we went on to begin the act with Pascale and, as we expected, the act was very popular with the audiences.

Of course, the truth was that we had Barny with us all along! (I might have been a magician for all the skill I was acquiring in making Barny appear and disappear!) I took him out of hiding after a week, as if he had just arrived, and offered to do the act with him as per our contract. But Mr Ton, the boss, said, "No, no, I like to watch Pascale work."

The main show in the Friedrichstadtpalast theatre was called "City Lights" and incorporated in it was a horse act. To accommodate such an act, a circus ring, hidden under the enormous stage, could be lifted into place in a matter of seconds by hydraulic jacks. The act in question was a high-school dressage riding act with two lady riders. One of them began to experience problems with one of the horses. My agent, who knew about my horse background, asked if I could fix things. After riding the misbehaving horse a few times, I was able to rectify his problems and help the rider to adapt to my improvement in the horse's behaviour.

The reputation I gained from this episode made me the prime candidate for solving the next problem that came up: the other girl in the act gave notice that she'd be leaving in three weeks' time. The act's contract stated "girls only", but another girl with the right experience to take her place couldn't be found in time and the act was again in jeopardy of being pulled from the show.

I wouldn't have thought of it on my own, but Pascale came to me. Looking me straight in the eye, she said, "I want to ride in the act."

I told her that wasn't a good idea, but she insisted, so in the end I gave in and told the dressage rider of our plan. She didn't have much choice and was happy to accept my help, so she gave the go-ahead for me to start Pascale's crash course in equestrian art. Since Pascale had seldom even been on a horse, I knew we had a big job ahead of us.

We worked terribly hard in the time left. Unfortunately, I even managed to get Pascale quite distressed on some occasions. My way of teaching is left over from the old school, where there's no room for pussyfooting around, and if Pascale didn't want to make a fool of herself on her debut as an equestrian artist, our marital status would have to be left out of the training area. It would be done my way, with no punches pulled.

In the beginning, Pascale couldn't quite get the hang of a particular dressage movement the horse was supposed to execute. To help her, I tried to think of a way to convey to Pascale how to give a certain signal or aid to the horse with her legs and the reins. I was still struggling with this problem right when it was time for the act's debut. We were in a private room just offstage, and Pascale was wearing her riding costume, complete with habit, boots and spurs. All of a sudden, I thought of a way to make my point clear and told her to get down on all fours. She did, under much protest. I straddled her, took off my scarf, looped it through her mouth, to more protests – muffled this time. I held the scarf as if it were reins and in this posture proceeded to give Pascale the aids I would give to a horse to get it to perform the correct manoeuvre.

Just then one of the American male singers from the show came into the room, and his eyes nearly popped out of his head. "Oops, sorry," he said, and hurried from the room before I could explain. (Some days later, Pascale passed him on the way to the dressing rooms, whereupon he whispered to her, "Oh, you French people.")

But Pascale demonstrated that she had plenty of grit – she came through my no-holds-barred training, learned what she had to do and didn't disappoint anyone at her debut and during the subsequent performances – she pulled it off marvellously. I don't know how we did it, but we did!

After we were settled into the engagement and the act was going well with no fear of us being fired, there was some time left for sightseeing. Usually sightseeing didn't interest me that much, but this time I wanted to go to the places I remembered when Berlin had been still divided.

We took a stroll down to the place where I recalled Checkpoint Charlie had been and were amazed to find nothing there except an open space. I remembered the hut-like construction where I had had to change my twenty Deutschmarks for twenty East German marks before crossing over from West to East, and all the other small outbuildings that had, among other things, presumably housed border guards.

I remembered the opening in the concrete wall, specially constructed so the cars had to zig-zag to get through. My gaze fell on a spot a few feet away, then I looked up about fifty yards further across the now open space. Turning to Pascale, I said, "Imagine, only a few years ago, anybody foolish enough to try and make a dash to freedom over this now-open space would have risked being shot to death." Maybe it didn't have this same impact on the people who lived here and experienced first-hand the gradual process of the wall coming down, and East and West Germany reuniting. But for me it was a shock, and instead of elation, I felt a chill at being able to witness this now open piece of land that showed no trace of its infamous past. *What a crazy, stupid era*, I thought to myself as we made our way back to the theatre.

*

Before coming to Berlin, I had realised that the simple routine we had done for the TV programme in Italy was not enough. The act needed something more stunning – a gag guaranteed to grab the audience's attention right at the beginning. I remembered once seeing a sketch that the great comic Benny Hill had done. In the sketch, he stepped over the handles of a handcart similar to ours just at the moment when somebody put something heavy on the other end, sending that end crashing down, and like a see-saw the handle end shot up, seemingly to hit Mr Hill in the crotch. I thought it was good slapstick comedy that fitted the dog act routine perfectly.

It took me surprisingly little time to train Bush to do his part. It entailed him coming out of the trunk and jumping up onto the cart at the opposite end from the handles just as I began to unload the luggage. I was standing with my back to the trunk, with my feet on either side of one of the handles. The handle end of the cart swung up, apparently catching me between my legs. During the trick, I had to stand well back towards the spot where the handle joined the rest of the cart to avoid it really hitting me – the further forward I was, the higher the travel of the handle on its upwards movement. This whole episode took only a few seconds to unfold, and before I could turn around, Bush was back in the trunk, out of sight. The sequence continued, as I played to the public's delight at my misfortune by making appropriate comical gestures. Pascale, who was facing the other way and hadn't seen this happen, came to my side. Then Bush came out of the trunk a second time to do the same gag. This time it was Pascale's turn to be the fall guy and the handle seemingly hit her in the backside. She turned round to face me, thinking I was the culprit, and proceeded to give me a pretend slap. She then left the scene in a huff. I hunched my shoulders in a gesture to the audience, as if to say, "What did I do?" Then I carried on with the normal routine.

For eighteen years Barny had pulled the cart, with me on it, into the ring or onto a stage somewhere. Although I knew in my heart that the new version of the act with Pascale was the best way to go for the future, it wasn't an easy decision to retire him. It was almost the only life he knew, and we continued to bring him along with us on engagements and put him up in a stable wherever we happened to be working. He never took part in the act again; however, he was hauled out of retirement once to work in front of a theatre audience in the centre of Munich, Germany, where we were booked with the dog act.

Although the programme was made up mainly of vaudeville acts, the theme and the way the show was choreographed gave it a circus theme. To give a bit more animal content and add to the circus flavour, the boss of the theatre asked us if Barny could be used in the finale of the show. Together with the rest of the cast, all he had to do was enter the front of the theatre and parade up through the aisles in the auditorium, then walk up two steps onto the stage. Barny enjoyed playing his part immensely.

To prepare for this stunt, Pascale, complete in her elegant lady outfit, had to lead Barny from behind the theatre out into the street and round to the front entrance. As it happened, the theatre was situated right in the middle of the city opposite the famous Hofbrauhaus beer hall. At that hour there weren't many people about except the late-night revellers, who exited the beer hall after an evening of merriment with arms linked, singing Bavarian beer drinking songs and swaying from side to side as they swilled down more litres of Munich brew. During the finale one night, I followed Pascale and I saw a man who was obviously quite drunk stumble out onto the sidewalk. Upon on seeing the strange apparition of Pascale and a donkey walking by, he shook his head in bewilderment and went straight back inside.

Pascale's successful participation in our theatre work made me realise that calling the act "Mike Sanger" literally didn't fit the bill any longer. So we decided to call ourselves "The Sangers".

*

Our theatre work set the trend for the kind of places in which we would perform over the next few years. The only circus work we did was the occasional short winter engagement. The circus way of life I described earlier that had captured my youthful zest for adventure had given way to a mellowing appreciation for a quieter life. Circus life is wonderful on the days when the sun was shining and we did only one performance a day, but most of the shows required putting on several performances per day, and generally the life had become harder over the years. Parking in muddy fields, hooking up the trailer for water and electricity and doing other chores in the rain while trying to get ready for a performance at the same time was tiring me, and I took happily to the relatively clean environment of working on stage.

In no way is this meant to disparage the way Dad did the act with his donkey or the many years I did the act with Barny as my loyal partner. It was right for that era, especially for the circus ring, which had to cater to a family audience. But now, Pascale's contribution gave the act the touch of sophistication needed for a more mature audience. It broadened the scope of places in which we could perform, enabling us to work almost anywhere. We began doing gala shows for the same agency that booked acts for the Lido in Paris.

We worked in many interesting venues and on many special occasions, one of which was performing in gala performances for Jacques Chirac at the Hotel de Ville when he was Mayor of Paris, and again one year later at the Palais de l'Élysée after he had become the French president.

On another occasion, we performed at the Opéra de Paris in the presence of Lionel Jospin, then Prime Minister of France. We were the only vaudeville act from the programme to be invited to a reception that evening at the Prime Minister's official residence, the Hôtel de Matignon. On each of these special occasions, regardless of political beliefs, I felt privileged to meet personally with those heads of state. I felt it was a tribute to the quality of the act that we were given the opportunity to visit such esteemed locales.

We were also doing more TV work. One notable date was performing with the French TV personality Patrick Sébastien, filmed in the Paris studios of TF 1. The show was called *Garcon, la Suite* and was notable for us because it was the first time we had done something with artists who were household names in France, not to mention international stars such as Nana Mouskouri.

*

Besides acquiring the dogs necessary for the act, our animal family occasionally grew larger when we took in a stray. We didn't go out of our way to find homeless animals, but now and again a situation would present itself in which we felt we had to do something or the animal would be doomed to live in misery or to die. The first such addition had been Lisa. I found her about the same time Pascale and I first got to know each other.

Lisa was a mutt about thirteen to fourteen years old, twelve inches high with a brown coat. I found her in a pitiful state, staggering along a road in Marseille. Pascale and I took her to a veterinarian, who said she wouldn't have lasted one more day out in the heat.

We adopted her and she took well to her new life and caring family. Once we nearly lost her. Somehow, unknown to us, the door of our living trailer had come open at some point during the journey. When we stopped at an autostrada toll booth in Italy, Lisa must have jumped out. As luck would have it, just as I was driving away, I happened to look into the rear-view mirror. At first glance, from a distance, I thought, *My goodness, that dog looks like Lisa.* Unaware of the open door, I prepared to drive on when, in one more glance, I noticed the dog had Lisa's characteristic way of walking, which made her look a bit like a waddling duck. We stopped immediately and went back to pick her up. Lisa lived with us for another three years before dying of old age.

Then, during an engagement at a theme park in Germany, a cat came to us. We later named him Hansi. Our contract with the park provided us with a ground floor apartment to live in. Hansi appeared one day and tapped with his paws on the glass-panelled door leading in from a small garden. The dogs didn't seem to mind, so we let him in and gave him some food. After he ate, he curled up on a couch and went to sleep for the rest of the day. This ritual repeated itself every day.

The only dog we had who could have posed a threat to Hansi was Chully. With his still-fierce character, he would certainly have attacked Hansi if he could have found him, but he was suffering with cataracts at that time and couldn't see very well. Chully could smell the cat, though, and sometimes tried to find him, but Hansi always managed to keep out of his way.

When the last day of the season at the park drew near, we were still undecided what to do about Hansi. We had vacated the apartment and moved back into our living trailer, which was located some distance away. Pascale had left some things in the apartment, and also we wanted to find out where Hansi was, so we drove back in the evening. Arriving at the back entrance, we saw Hansi tapping away at the door to the now-dark, empty apartment. It was a cold night with a near-freezing drizzle coming down. The touching sight of Hansi trying to get in made up our minds, and we took him in to become a permanent member of the family.

Another dog became one of the family after I bought him as a puppy with the intention of training him for the act. Unfortunately, I made a mistake in judging his size, and when he was fully grown, he was too small for the big dog's role in the act and too big for the small dog's role. It was my mistake, and accepting my responsibility for having given him a home in the first place, we couldn't bear to part with him and kept him as a pet. He became the second Patchy, named after my first small dog.

In between stage and TV, we did accept an offer one winter to go to a circus in Lisbon, Portugal, for a short Christmas season. It was a long journey from Normandy, so instead of hauling our living trailer, which would slow us down somewhat, we decided to leave it behind and rent somewhere to live when we arrived, for the duration of the engagement. When we got there, we found a campground just outside the city which had clean, well-equipped bungalows for hire. The circus provided us with a light utility truck to transport us and the dogs to and from the circus building, which was located in the centre of the city. Every day we drove into town for the performances and back to the campground again at night.

As we grew familiar with our new surroundings in the campsite, we became aware of a number of stray dogs roaming around. Some of the staff put food out for them. One evening as we drove back through the entrance, we noticed one dog who, apart from the cowed, defeated look that most strays have, seemed to be in a sorrier state than the others. The dog was white with brown markings and resembled a Lévrier or Whippet mix.

"Let's have a closer look," said Pascale.

Getting nearer, we noticed that the dog was limping along on three legs, with the right hind leg trailing helplessly. Before we could get any closer, the dog hopped out of sight and it was the last we saw of the poor animal that evening. The next day, driving out of the gate, we saw the dog again. In daylight we got a better look and were horrified to see a bloody gash at the top of its leg with some bone protruding. I stopped and rolled down the window. A uniformed campsite worker was emptying trash cans nearby. Luckily, he spoke some English, and I asked if he knew anything about the dog. The man told us that two or three weeks ago a co-worker had seen the dog thrown from a moving car on the road in front of the campsite, and seconds later another vehicle hit the dog and broke its leg. Some people from the campsite had brought the ailing animal into the site and were providing food, but that was all.

"I think it's a female," the man added.

The next day it was pouring rain. Keeping a lookout for the dog, I drove slowly as we made our way through the campsite towards the exit.

"There she is," Pascale cried out.

The dog was hopping around near one of the administration buildings. We stopped and got out. When we walked towards her, she came to us with head bowed low and began wagging her tail. She let us caress her, and looked at us in a demure way, as if asking us to take pity on her. We stayed with her for a while longer, then I looked at my watch and realised we might be late for the performance. Reluctantly, we left her there, staring after us in the rain.

We didn't talk much on the trip downtown. I knew Pascale well enough to know she was struggling with the same thoughts as I was. Our limited space was precious, and we should only consider taking dogs that would be candidates for the act.

Later, preparing ourselves for the performance, we discussed the dog and it was evident that whatever problems would arise, Pascale was resolved in her determination to save her. I had to agree – I couldn't turn my back on her either. Dogs had provided me with a living and way of life that I loved. Saving one provided me with a small way to repay them.

When we arrived back at the campsite late that night, we found her out in the open, curled up on a patch of grass with no protection from the driving rain. Presumably, she didn't have the will to seek out a more sheltered place. It was a sign of resignation to her fate. We hurried to see what we could do for her. The leg wound glistened an angry red, likely infected. The piece of bone sticking out was polished white by the pounding rain. She had a dull look in her eyes and the slow way she raised her head told me she probably had a high temperature. Her condition since that morning had changed dramatically. Something had to be done quickly, otherwise it would be too late.

"We have to get her to a vet," Pascale said.

"The sooner the better," I replied. "Just give me time to take Bush and Tacki home and see to the others and I'll rejoin you here."

After working quickly to see to the other dogs' needs, I rushed back to Pascale and the little bitch. I always kept a spare collar for emergencies, so I slipped it over her head and led her to the truck. She was handicapped by the bad leg and far too weak to jump inside herself. Being careful not to bang the leg I lifted her inside through the sliding door at the back.

We managed to find an emergency animal clinic. Portuguese is not one of my languages, but luckily, the veterinarian spoke French and English. He took X-rays and told us the fracture was bad and couldn't be operated on until the infection had been brought under control. He proceeded to make a thorough examination and clean the wound. After the leg was cleaned and dressed in a thick bandage, he told us he would operate to set the broken bones in a few days; however, the healing process could be difficult because the break had gone so long unattended, which could impair the fusing of the bones.

Although the dog must have been in considerable pain, I was amazed at how calm she stayed throughout the visit. I think, foremost, it was courage, but also a feeling of confidence in what we were doing for her. Whatever it was, she gave herself willingly to all the manoeuvring, prodding and manipulating by the vet.

By the time we left the clinic and found a pharmacy open for the antibiotics, it was late. When we arrived home, Pascale put some food down for her; she ate slowly but still managed to finish it. Then, we fixed a blanket for her in the kitchen and, sensing it was for her, the dog limped over to it and flopped down on the side of her good leg. The tranquil gaze she fixed on me was a silent thank you, and when I stroked her and murmured, "Good girl," she lowered her head to the soft folds of the blanket.

Before we went to bed, Pascale thought of a name for her. The idea came from a phone call we had received earlier in the day from an agent. He had informed us that he'd sent a video of the act to the Big Apple Circus in New York City, in hopes of securing work for us there.

"Apple would be a nice name," Pascale said.

The antibiotics began to take effect, and along with the help of good food and rest in a warm place, her condition quickly improved. Her eyes grew brighter and she regained strength. Now it remained to be seen what could be done for the leg. There was no circus performance the day of the operation, so with time to spare it didn't bother us to find a lot of people in the animal clinic waiting room. However, I soon became concerned. Pet owners were being called into the doctor's room one after the other; these appeared to be normal consultation hours. We thought for a big thing like an operation, the dog should be dropped off early in the morning, then if everything went well, collected later on in the day. The situation at the clinic made it appear as if Apple was going to have the operation squeezed between other mundane consultations. Compared to our previous experiences at animal clinics, it made the situation seem a bit makeshift, and I was worried for Apple's sake. Pascale voiced the same concern.

"But it's the first time we've been to Portugal, maybe that's how things are done here," she added.

Moments later, our name was called. I looked at Pascale, she looked at me, each of us silently asking the other to take the initiative – either to call it off or say let's do it. Neither of us had the answer. I acted on impulse when I took a grip on Apple's lead and led her towards the door held open by the vet's assistant.

Taking Apple she said, "This will take a while, you can either wait outside or I suggest you go and drink a coffee somewhere and come back in about an hour." Before we left, Pascale gave Apple a reassuring embrace.

An hour later, Apple was still groggy from the anaesthetic when we picked her up. We asked what we owed for the operation.

"Nothing," said the doctor. And then it became clear – the meagrely equipped operating room and the clinic's makeshift way of doing things. Unbeknownst to us, the night when we first went looking for an emergency animal clinic in the heavy rain, we had been directed to a special clinic that dealt with homeless animals, where the veterinary doctors, working in rotation, gave their services free.

It was the last week before we left to go back home to France, and I didn't like the look of the wound. The vet had left a drain hole between the stitches, where a stainless-steel pin had been put in place to hold the bones together. That pin was barely visible, but after a few days I noticed that the pin shifted every time Apple moved the leg.

No way is it going to heal properly, I thought to myself.

We decided not to seek any more treatment for her in Lisbon; we'd wait until we got home to our veterinary clinic in a town near to us.

With the exception of Mitzi, the other dogs had accepted Apple into our family. Mitzi, on the other hand, looked at Apple suspiciously, growling whenever she came near. Mitzi had been the only female up to that time, and even though Apple was handicapped by a bad leg, Mitzi saw her as a rival – not only for the other dogs' attention but also for Pascale's affection. Pascale was devoted to Mitzi and with hugs, she reassured her that, apart from Bush, Mitzi was the main one in her life. She gently stroked her and tried to explain that Apple was a poor sick stray that needed help.

It took us two days to make the trip home, and we took Apple to our regular veterinary clinic, one of the best clinics I know. The vet most experienced in fixing broken bones took on Apple's case. He took X-rays and after studying them for some minutes, his first reaction was to advise us that the leg should be amputated.

"There is a necrosis of the bone – in more simple terms, a mortification of the bone. The bone is going rotten. If we decide to go all out to save the leg, I will have to cut some of the bone away, reset it with the help of metal pins, then hope for the best; however, I don't give it much chance." The vet didn't need to pussyfoot with us and knew we appreciated his honesty. When he learned how we had come upon Apple, he offered to give us a reduction on the cost of the operation. Whatever the cost, we decided to try and save the leg, so the operation was scheduled in two days.

Taking three and a half hours, the operation was a much more elaborate affair than the one in Lisbon. Afterwards, over the next three weeks, we took Apple to the clinic for frequent check-ups. During those visits her quiet, courageous character, void of any protest to all the treatment being dished out, began to win the hearts of the vet and the staff. Whenever we arrived at the clinic, everybody made a fuss over her.

For all their efforts, the next set of X-rays showed that the bones were not fusing together. Resigned to acknowledging defeat, we braced ourselves to give consent for the leg to be amputated. However, the vet, in a complete reversal of his rather negative outlook in the beginning, took on Apple's case as his own personal crusade to save the leg. He told us he'd been in contact with a university clinic and, in delving into their archives of past cases similar to Apple's, had found among many failures also some successful outcomes. He wanted to try just one more operation.

To find healthy bone, which would have a better chance to knitting together, the procedure required him to measure the bone exactly to know the maximum he could cut away at both ends (it was explained to me there is an exact percentage of the total length that must not be exceeded). This meant the leg would be somewhat shorter than the hind right, but in his view Apple would adapt to it. We consented, and he went ahead with another lengthy operation.

"Poor Apple," Pascale said, "if this doesn't work, she'll lose the leg, and all the suffering has been for nothing."

They kept Apple at the clinic for a couple of days after the operation. Before we took her home, the vet told us to let him know the moment she started to put weight on the leg. Two weeks went by with no improvement. Then one day, as the other dogs and Apple were playing around, I noticed that she touched the ground a couple of times with that bad leg. It caught me by surprise and, not wanting to miss anything, I concentrated my attention on her. Sure enough, now and again, as she hopped around, she attempted to sprint away after the other dogs with the help of the bad leg. I didn't want to build any false hopes, so I waited until the next day to make sure there was a definite improvement before notifying the clinic.

I was overjoyed when Apple used the leg more the next day and put some weight on it. At the end of the next week she was using the leg more often and at the end of two months it had become nearly as muscular as the other hind leg. The leg had been saved. We thanked the vet, who was overjoyed and quite rightly proud of his efforts.

And, to top it off, not only did Apple retain her leg, but she became famous in veterinary annals – her case is now on file as a reference in a veterinary teaching university clinic.

*

During this period we were constantly finding ways to upgrade the act. My character had changed to a bell-boy. Pascale had an elegant Aubrey Hepburn *Breakfast at Tiffany's* look, complete with large hat. We had our costumes custom-made by the finest theatrical tailor in Paris.

Also, for a long time we'd been searching for a way to include Pascale in the entire act. We mentioned this to a friend.

"After Pascale slaps you, she could go and sit at a table. That way she would complement the chic hotel lobby ambiance that fits the routine so well."

The idea was simple and so right that I felt stupid for not having thought of it myself. Pascale's inclusion in the rest of the act gave me the opportunity to add some more gags without affecting the dogs' routine or the need to train them to do something extra.

Neither did the props escape our attention. To replace the handcart I had hastily put together for the Italian TV show, we had a new one made that was fabricated of polished stainless steel that glinted in the spotlights.

Two items I couldn't improve on were the suitcases. They were standing up well to the rigors of being thrown about during the act and the constant wear and tear of travelling from one engagement to another. We had done well to choose the best quality leather for their fabrication. When I cleaned them now and again with saddle soap, they came out looking like new.

Bush and Tacki made things easy for me; there was no need to practise them any more. They had reached a stage of professionalism that was astounding. Sometimes, even after experiencing a long break in between contracts, we would arrive at an engagement and without any preparation and in all kinds of conditions – stage, TV studio, open air or whatever – they were happy to get going again, performing exuberantly and faultlessly. Thanks to them and all the improvements we had made, the act was enjoying an extended period of success and we were gradually gaining a foothold in a more sophisticated side of show business.

Looking to the future, we began to search for an eventual replacement for Bush. I wanted to take a dog from a shelter, so we visited as many as we could. I'm like most animal lovers when I go to a dogs' home. I want to take them all with me, especially the sad-looking ones. I remember going to one where they had rows of kennels, each designated with a number. I can't remember exactly how the system worked, but it was something like this: row one was for the newcomers who had seven days to find a home before being put to sleep, row two had just six days left, right down to row six, where the dogs had just one more day.

Whether this policy was always adhered to I don't know – and indeed, maybe it had been set up so as to make the public more willing to take a dog out of row six. It had touched a sentimental chord in me when I earlier took Kelly and later Bush from such situations. On each occasion I made a silent pledge to give them love, care and attention for the rest of their lives, or for as long as I was able.

In our present quest, even after an exhaustive search in all the local kennels, I just couldn't find the right dog for the act. I knew I had to have one trained ready to coincide with retiring Bush, and was beginning to despair of finding one in time.

"If we can't find the right dog in a shelter, maybe I should look more toward a particular breed," I said.

Pascale replied, "Kelly was so good at doing the act, why not a Hovawart?"

I still wanted to give some needy animal a home; nevertheless, it had to be the right one and dogs like Bush were hard to find. Finally, after looking in one more dog pound to no avail, I agreed with her to look for a Hovawart. It was a lucky moment to make that decision, because we were working in an amusement park in the north of Germany. Our location would make it easier to track down a suitable puppy of this German breed.

The syllable "hov" in the name means "court", as in courtyard. The name "wart" means guard, or guardian. Thus the entire name of the breed had the elegant meaning, "Guardian of the Court". That's how I believe the name originated.

One difference this time, in comparison to how we found Kelly, would be that I could choose the dog's colour. I thought the blond or golden type would be better-looking for show business.

We found loads of breeders in a monthly dog magazine, and a few of them announced that their bitches were either expecting or had just had pups. We singled out a couple of breeders that were quite local and made the necessary phone calls for appointments to see them.

The first place we went had a litter of six pups, but four of them had already been allocated to owners and the two remaining ones were bitches. I was looking for a male. The next dogs we went to see were located way out in the country at a big house with an adjoining stable block for horses. From the look of the place, I thought the people must be well off. As it turned out, the lady of the house bred Hovawarts just as a hobby. She led us to the stable. She kept the female dog with her new puppies in one of the horse boxes. One of the puppies interested us. He was the smallest of the bunch, but also the liveliest, and carried his tail sticking straight up. To me, that is always a good sign. The only thing that worried me slightly was that the mother was very shy, and if he happened to inherit that trait, I could forget training him for the act. He would be no good at all for working in front of an audience.

We asked if we could see the father, and luckily enough, although he wasn't on the actual premises, he lived not too far away. The lady made a quick phone call to the owner to make sure it was convenient for us to come and pay a visit, and after getting directions we were on our way.

The owners had a bakery in a small village in a heavily wooded area. The people were very hospitable and seemed to enjoy showing off their prime Hovawart. He was not the least bit shy, and although he was seven years old, he played around like a puppy. If we hadn't seen the father, I don't think we would have taken the risk of buying that puppy. But having done so, and knowing that his father was gregarious, with a lively disposition, we decided to bring the puppy into our family and try to make a star out of him. We hoped our puppy would take after his father and not inherit his mother's shyness. We called him Altan.

Not long after finding Altan we experienced a loss in our dog family. At fourteen, Chully succumbed to a bout of pneumonia. He'd been on antibiotics for two weeks, and instead of getting better, he got worse. Once again we had to take the unhappy decision, and Chully was put to sleep. It was an agonising moment, when right to the last, true to his fighting character, he tried to bite the plastic tube that carried the euthanasia fluid into his veins. We would miss our feisty, fearless little friend.

Although we were finding well-paid work in fancy places, the downside of giving up circus work was that occasionally we had to wait months before the next engagement came along. Therefore, ironically, our elevation in status and quality resulted in a hand-to-mouth kind of living for us. Nonetheless, I felt it was just a period we had to endure until the act was better known in our new environment of stage and cabaret.

*

Six months later, we were on the road, driving up to Paris from Normandy. Springtime was in full bloom, the weather was lovely and it was unusually warm for that time of year. Although I felt a little apprehensive about the trip we were about to make, I was in good spirits. I thought Pascale was probably feeling the same way. Admittedly, she was a bit quiet, but I put that down to fatigue from packing the night before.

Now, as we stood in the busy departure lounge at Orly airport, I realised it wasn't just tiredness, because Pascale broke down in tears. I thought the Royal Air Maroc official was going to get down on his hands and knees to plead with us to board the plane. The dog act props were littering the departure lounge in front of the check-in area, and a string of passengers were looking on with expressions ranging from surprise to disgust at the show of emotion. The only ones who seemed to be enjoying themselves were Bush, who had an almost-human grin on his face, and Tacki, whose tail was wagging in anticipation. They were excited at the prospect of a trip somewhere.

I imagined what might be going through the head of the airline official. "These people are destined to perform for the King, and it's my responsibility to see they are on the flight – otherwise dire things may happen to me. Oh, why don't they make up their minds?"

It was the first time we had flown to any engagement with the dogs, and Pascale was getting last-minute jitters, worried that the dogs might be put on the wrong plane or in the wrong hold, or that something else might happen that would put them at risk. Her mood had penetrated my fragile confidence, and I wasn't sure what to do.

We went outside to calm down and make our minds up, leaving the RAM man fretting over what was going to happen to him. Pascale didn't really want to go, but I reasoned with her that we needed this work and we couldn't back down now. Finally she agreed, and we went back inside and gave the good news to the poor airline official. Straight away a whole army of airport workers descended on the props, carrying them through the check-in and whisking the dogs away in boxes.

That wasn't the end of our problems, though. Upon boarding the aircraft, we were informed there weren't any seats left for us – and Pascale couldn't disprove their claims, as she had lost the tickets. I started to panic, imagining us being put off the plane and the dogs ending up in Morocco without us. Things were sorted out at the last minute when the steward discovered why and for whom we were going to Morocco; two places were found for us in first class. I am certain, however, that Royal Air Maroc does not have fond memories of us.

The actual flight was uneventful, except for us both worrying whether the dogs were okay. On arrival, we were asked to wait until the other passengers had disembarked. When we finally left the plane, the dogs were brought out to us and were none the worse from the two-hour flight. To our surprise, parked in front of the aircraft waiting for us was a limousine and Chevy van, complete with chauffeurs. After loading the props and dogs into the van, we were ushered through customs with just a quick glance at our passports, then taken to our hotel. I rode in the van with the props and dogs, while Pascale rode in the car. The hotel was luxurious and we had a good night's sleep. And the dogs seemed quite happy with their air-conditioned comfort.

The next day I was running the dogs in front of the hotel when I noticed the same driver who had brought Pascale to the hotel standing in front of his car. I went over to say hello and asked him if he was waiting for anyone important. He informed me, with a look of surprise, that his orders were to be at our disposal for the entire time of our stay in Rabat. It was my turn to look surprised – I wasn't at all used to this degree of hospitality.

That afternoon we were driven to the palace to get ready for the show. I was a bit worried about the heat, but our dressing room was air-conditioned, so it wasn't uncomfortable for the dogs. We met the rest of the company who were booked for the show – they mainly consisted of an American clown troupe – then rehearsed for the show. The performance was being organised by the Moroccan ambassador to the USA as a birthday present for one of the King's granddaughters.

The boss of the clowns said to me, "I supply clowns. You need clowns, I've got 'em – hundreds of 'em, anytime, anywhere." He showed me his business card; it had "Clown Factory" written on it. I tried to imagine hundreds of clowns, and unbidden, the image of hundreds of clowns gliding by on a factory production line came into my mind.

As it was getting near showtime, I changed into my costume and took Bush and Tacki outside for a run before going to work. As we were strolling up and down, I noticed the guards standing around. They wore traditional Moroccan costume – white, with red fezzes – but what amazed me was how big and tall they were. None of the Moroccans I knew were anywhere near that size. And most impressively, they had bloody big cutlasses hanging at their sides (only an expression)!

Just then a Rolls Royce pulled up some distance from us and two gentlemen got out and started walking in our direction. They were very well dressed in western clothes. Now, I'd never seen any of the Moroccan royal family – only photographs of King Hassan. I didn't know who these two gentlemen were, but as they continued their way towards us, guards bowed to them and other people went down on one knee in front of them, kissing the back of their hands. Being of average intelligence, I was able to deduce that they were personages of some importance – and it looked as if they were coming to me! Well, I couldn't go down on one knee because I would make the costume dirty, so the least I could do was take off my hat, trying to make it look as if I was doing it for them and not to scratch my head. They obviously knew I had flown from France to do the show, and assumed that I was French.

"*Bonjour*," they said to me. "What are your dogs' names?"

"This is Bush, and the small one is Tacki," I told them in French. They both asked me questions about the dogs and what they would be doing later in the performance. As I speak French not too badly, I didn't try to change the language, even though I was sure they spoke English fluently. They patted the dogs and said goodbye to us. After they were out of sight, I turned to one of the guards, and asked who the two gentlemen were.

"They are the two princes."

"Oh my goodness! I hope I conducted myself in a proper manner."

"Well, it's a good thing you took your hat off," he replied.

Before we had left Paris, the agency who booked us warned that there was to be absolutely no attention whatsoever drawn to sexual parts in the performances. This meant, for instance, that Pascale was to wear a long dress covering her knees. The trick in which the handles of the handcart hit me in the crotch worried me a bit – especially when I thought of one of those guards wielding his cutlass in response to us not paying proper attention to Royal protocol. The agency also warned us there would be little response from the audience in the way of laughter or applause – fortunately, this turned out to be untrue. They proved to be a very warm public indeed. I went ahead with the bit where the wagon handle hits me in the crotch but tempered my reaction. Just like the rest of our act, it was met with audience approval and, as no guards came forward to behead me, I reckoned we had gotten through without offence.

Straight after the performance the King jumped up onto the stage and most enthusiastically shook each one of us by the hand, thanking us for the evening's entertainment.

We got back to the hotel with just enough time to feed Bush and Tacki, take them for a run and get changed before Pascale and I, along with the rest of the cast, were picked up by a posse of cars that took us to the ambassador's residence for dinner. Other than the palace, I have never seen a place more heavily guarded, but these guards lacked in class compared to the palace sentinels – they only had guns instead of cutlasses.

The ambassador was a charming host and the dinner was less formal than I had feared. A sumptuous meal attended to by servants plus the gaiety of the clowns made it an interesting evening. Conversation was lively, as quite a few of the clown troupe came from New York, where the ambassador had also lived for some time. I have since lived in New York for a short time and understand why there was so much to talk about. On parting, we were the recipients of a strange but most welcome gesture of hospitality; we were all given envelopes, each containing three hundred dollars.

The next morning found us at the airport for the flight home. This time we didn't experience near the level of anxiety we had on the journey out. The first time we had been sure that flying with the dogs would be a nasty business. Now that we had done it once, we felt we could do it again, and on the return flight we acted as if we were old hands.

5

SOMETIME LATER, BACK HOME IN NORMANDY, the phone rang and Pascale picked it up.

"Yes, we'll be free then," Pascale said. I heard her discuss prices and conditions for an engagement. Nearly three months had gone by since we had returned from Morocco and finances were getting strained – in fact, we were getting desperate for work. After Pascale hung up, she told me that the agency had made us an offer to go to a nightclub in Modena in northern Italy.

"Fine," I said. "The only problem is, we've never worked in a place like that – a nightclub is not the same as a cabaret." I wasn't sure our kind of comedy would go well with the clientele and the ambiance of a nightclub. I tried to imagine us working in between two strip acts. Nevertheless, it meshed with our plans to diversify the type of work we could get. If they wanted us, then what the hell, we should give it a try. We had two weeks before our start date in Italy and the very next day, we had another phone call from the agency, this time asking if we'd be interested in doing an audition for the Lido in Paris. I had heard from several people that it wasn't easy to work in the Lido from the point of view of audience response, especially for comedy. The feedback from the audience affects my timing in going from one gag to the next, and the Lido had a reputation of catering to a very sophisticated audience, who even if they liked something weren't likely to explode in laughter. That's why the club was cautious engaging a comedy act and wanted us to do an audition first, to be sure it was the kind of comedy that would appeal to their clientele.

Even knowing the probable difficulty of pleasing the audience, the Lido is somewhat of a mecca for show artists and I jumped at the chance to work there. The audition was set up for three days later.

Altan jumped up onto my lap, reminding me it was time for his training session. He was three quarters of the way through his training to be the backup dog for Bush. It had been eight years since we found Bush in Baden-Baden, and he had been the mainstay of the act ever since.

I used to do my training in the garden, which wasn't the ideal place, because Normandy is like England – it has a lot of inclement weather. Still, I had no choice. But I had had a bit of luck not long before when we did the act for charity in the local village hall. After the performance, I was speaking to Claude, a person on the village council, and told him of my problem having to train the dogs out in the garden. He immediately offered to let me use the village hall and gave me a set of keys so I could come and go as I pleased. Later on, I got the feeling that Claude was rather proud that international show artists were making use of his village hall – especially when I came back with stories of all the places where we had worked.

I grew to love that little place. It was like a church inside, and when I closed the doors behind me there was complete silence that enabled us to concentrate. Of course, for the dogs to be able to do their work and not be distracted by the audience, which sometimes can be quite noisy, it is desirable at some point in the training to get them used to distractions so they can still work efficiently. In the beginning, though, it's better to have quiet, with not so many people around. It has the effect of keeping the dog's concentration fully on me so he can notice any slightest signal I might use.

Training the dogs had become a way of life for me. It ran parallel to everything else I did, and over the years I honed my skills at it and perfected a system that guaranteed success in training the routine of the act. On reflection, I suppose I could write a whole manual on how to train dogs. However, to keep them happy in their work, and to allow them to continue to develop their own character and their own way of doing things during the training, it must go beyond just some kind of methodical system that one can put down in writing.

When first beginning, I just play with the dog. This allows us to get to know each other and to build a mutual trust. That leads to producing what I would call a dialogue between us, which forms the basis of the dog knowing through my voice and gestures more or less what I want him to do later on. Of course, that is confined to basics, as it would be foolish to suggest that through gestures alone I could tell a dog all in one go how he has to go and hide in the trunk. As an example, here is a simple trick I had to train Altan to do. Though simple, it does encompass all the basics of my training.

Altan had to learn to jump off the trunk where he'd been sitting, run over to a chair that I was about to sit on and pull it backwards. I use a folding chair that closes up on itself and collapses flat on the floor, so that I land on my backside (slapstick comedy). There are two things involved in this trick. The first is for Altan to know the actual moment to do it, and the second is to show him how to do it. It wouldn't be logical to train the timing bit first – that is to say, when to come and pull the chair. So I begin with the actual trick of him pulling the chair with his paws. I start by leading him from the trunk up to the chair, where for the first two or three days I just lift his front end up and place his paws on the backrest of the chair, telling him all the time what a good boy he is and gaining his confidence and showing him there is nothing disturbing about it. That's where all the playing and gaining an understanding between us comes in handy. Then, we progress to my gently pulling his paws backwards until the chair falls. That's when I have to be very careful that the chair never comes down on his legs, as being hurt in doing his part would be fatal to learning the trick. I do that a maximum of three times each training session. That goes on for days, weeks or however long it takes before he shows signs of taking the initiative and pulling on his own. That happens quite suddenly and unexpectedly sometimes. It must be of his own doing and not forced. Once that happens, we're on our way, and it's only a matter of time before he will do it completely on his own.

Each time he does the trick successfully, I shower him with "good boys", petting him and generally making a fuss over him. I don't feed him anything for doing it; I don't believe that dogs have to be bribed for doing a trick. I want them to do something because they like doing it, and I try to help them understand that we are a team, and what they are doing is a part of what our life together is about. I really do believe that is what I am capable of instilling in the dogs. To have a clear conscience, one of my priorities, ultimately, is for them to be happy, and I do believe I achieve that goal.

After the initial phase of Altan pulling the backrest of the chair backwards, I slowly move away. At first only a few inches at a time, until after what should only be a few days, I can take my position in front of the chair ready to sit down. During this time of letting him do the trick on his own, I start to cue or give a signal to him when he should come off the trunk and do the trick. The cue is something quite audible, like clapping with my hands or using arm gestures. It's all very conspicuous, but as things progress I can minimise all that, until in the end I do away with the clapping and arm waving entirely, and the signal becomes the moments leading up to the trick.

The key to a successful outcome is not to take any short cuts. Probably the most important thing is to know the right moment to go from one phase of the trick to the next.

To begin the training of a new dog, I take things slowly, but then the training takes on a momentum of its own that has to be kept up with. If I linger on a part of the trick when I should move on, that phase of training can become stale and entrenched. If I move on too quickly, something undone is left behind that can never be recovered. In my view, all parts of this process could be learned from a book except that understanding of when to progress and move on to each next stage of the trick. That has to come from an inborn instinct which in time matures with experience gained by trial and error.

Another important aspect is not to allow any change in what I do. The dogs have to know me for what I am and feel comfortable with me at all times. In actual fact, the training becomes like a religious discipline. You have to keep your emotions and moods in check. That's where training in the little hall helped, as it was so calm and peaceful there. It helped reinforce my contact with Altan at a critical time in his training. He was making slow progress at the moment, but I knew I couldn't rush things. One of the traits of his breed is they keep their puppy ways longer than most others. Altan was living up to this, and it was preventing us from breaking into the stage where, although the work is still a fun thing, it also becomes a professional thing where the dog comes to understand it has to be done on a regular basis. Altan got bored sometimes and sulked like a spoiled child, so I had to find a balance of humouring him and still maintaining the necessary discipline to carry out the routine of the act – real character-building stuff, not only for him but also for me. I had to tap into reserves of patience I didn't know I had.

Another point to keep in mind is that in between training sessions, it's necessary to analyse what happened in the last one, so as to decide how best to tackle the next. I wanted to make the most of having the hall to train in before leaving for Italy, but in the meantime, I still had to prepare for the audition at the Lido with Bush and Tacki.

*

The preparation for the Lido was more in the way of making sure the props were clean and looking good, and that the music CD was sure to work okay. The costumes were Pascale's department.

Our car at the time was a Ford Sierra, with not enough room inside for the dogs and the props. Yet our truck would be a little too large to park in the street at the back of the Lido near the stage door. We decided to hire a Renault Espace. It would also give us a bit more class for the occasion. When we arrived at the appointed time, there were no free parking spaces by the stage door. We double-parked, unloaded everything, then went some distance before finding a parking spot for the Espace. Inside the Lido, we met our agent Liliane and set up the props.

I thought the audition went rather well. The dogs were wonderful, and Pascale and I did our best. Only the music could have gone better, because the sound technician didn't change to the different tunes that correspond to the four phases of the act at the right moments. However, that had always been a problem for us when we only had a few minutes beforehand to give instructions.

Although the Lido people seemed to like the act, we had to satisfy ourselves with at least having done the audition but without any clear commitment from them for an engagement, at least not for the near future. Renting the Renault had used up money badly needed for other expenses, so we would have to arrive at Modena on our last resources. This job was beginning to seem very important. Then I came up with an idea to make things easier for us.

The previous year we had worked at the Gardaland Amusement Park, situated on the shores of Lake Garda, not far from Verona.

Modena was only an hour's drive from there. During our season in the Park, Pascale and I had become friends with a local man; I will call him Antonio. He offered to let us stay at his place not only during our engagement but any time we wished.

I told Pascale of my plan, explaining that we could base ourselves at Antonio's place and commute to Modena each evening for the show. We both agreed that even after offering to pay for our needs, such as electricity and water, it would be less expensive and more pleasant than staying in a campground. And we'd be amongst friends. Both Pascale and I thought, at that time, that we were on the verge of a breakthrough as far as work was concerned. It was taking a hell of a long time for us to get regular engagements in the gala, cabaret and variety-show kind of work that we wanted to do, but finally, the situation seemed to be getting better. The quality of the shows we were being offered was excellent. Also the prospect of working at the Lido was very exciting for us.

In the meantime, I learned that the club in Modena was considered to be one of the top nightspots in the whole of Italy. I thought the scarcity of work coming to us had no reflection on the quality of the act but was more a question of us becoming known as a reliable attraction for those kinds of venues. I felt that the more engagements we completed successfully, the quicker the work would come in.

The day after returning from Paris, I began preparing for the journey to Italy. I was a little apprehensive about the trip because of the condition of our vehicles. The long gaps between engagements was affecting our budget for the two vehicles. Apart from the Ford, we had a Renault truck to pull our living trailer which also gave us extra room for the dogs. We really needed a new one, but this one would have to last a bit longer, at least until we started getting more work on a regular basis.

I phoned Antonio to ask if it was convenient to stay at his place. Actually, when I say his place, it wasn't technically his, because he still lived with his parents. This also goes some way in explaining what kind of a character Antonio was.

I first met Antonio while working in Gardaland. Because of my previous work with horses and the interest I still harboured for riding, I went to visit a local riding school. After riding one of the horses there, I noticed a man who kept watching me and smiling. He was of medium build, somewhere in his thirties and wore jeans, a bit faded but well pressed, and a blue open-necked shirt. He had short dark hair and wire-rimmed, John Lennon-type glasses. I remembered seeing him just before I started to ride the horse and noticed that other people from the riding school were greeting him like some long-lost son. Then he started following me around, and I began to think he was a little strange. Finally, while I was looking at some of the horses in the stable block, he came and spoke to me.

"*Buongiorno, sono Antonio.*"

"*Buongiorno, sono Mike,*" I replied in a reserved sort of way.

"I didn't want to impose myself on you, but I noticed how you ride differently from the other people here. They do mainly jumping and just riding for pleasure. You mount a horse like a dressage rider."

"That's possible," I said, "because I did most of my riding in Germany, riding high school and sitting on a horse the dressage way."

Antonio told me he'd kept his horse at the riding school up until last year, but then had to sell him because of family problems. He didn't elaborate on what those problems were, and I didn't press him on the matter. He went on to say that today was the first time he'd been back to the riding school since selling his horse, and it brought back a lot of memories that made him sad.

"If I still had my horse, I would like to go to Germany to study under one of the great masters of dressage riding," Antonio said.

His interest in that discipline of horsemanship was evidently what compelled him to want to talk to me. Our conversation continued about horses and riding. I told him where we were working, and he said he sometimes visited Gardaland. Then he told me how he had agonised over the decision to sell his horse.

Antonio is one of those people who have a permanent smile. Even as he was telling me about his horse and how much he missed him, he didn't lose his smile. Later, as I got to know him and understand him better, I knew Antonio's continual smile and penchant for following me around was just his way of doing things.

I sensed this was a lonely person and told him if he wanted to, he could come and visit us at the campsite where we were staying. Antonio shook my hand vigorously. He seemed overwhelmed at my friendly gesture and wouldn't stop thanking me. Right from that first meeting, there was something about Antonio that made him stand out as different from anybody I have ever known. When I made that offer to him, I didn't realise how quickly he'd take me up on it.

That evening, I had taken the dogs out for their last run of the day. As we prepared for bed, the dogs started to bark. They quieted down for a few minutes, but then started up again. So I went outside to see if someone was prowling around. A few yards away, I saw Antonio, standing meekly with his head bowed and his perpetual smile, looking towards our trailer. When he saw me, his smile broadened.

I called out to him, "It's a bit late, but never mind. Don't just stand there. Come inside."

"I am sorry to disturb you at this hour," he said.

"As long as it doesn't become a habit," I replied, deadpan.

Antonio smiled ingratiatingly, and we entered the trailer. I introduced him to Pascale and the two of them got into a lively discussion about his horse and what we did for a living. Our way of life and how the dogs were trained and performed fascinated him.

After that first encounter, he showed up occasionally without notice. Sometimes we saw him every day for a week or so, then for some reason or other, not for weeks on end.

Initially after leaving Gardaland, we kept in touch regularly, but gradually lost contact. However, when I phoned from Normandy to ask if we could come to stay for the duration of our contract in Modena, he sounded genuinely pleased to hear from me again and told us we would be more than welcome to come and stay. I asked him if it would be okay with his parents, and he assured me it would be.

We began to plan the journey, looking forward to the new engagement and being in a new location; we also looked forward to seeing Antonio once again.

*

In planning for our journey, I decided to go east towards Paris, then south to Lyon, skirting the Swiss border near Geneva and passing through the Mont Blanc tunnel into Italy. The whole trip would take at least two days with an overnight stop, which wouldn't be a problem, as I could just pull over and take a few hours' nap in the trailer. Pascale would leave one day after I did, driving the Ford. Before leaving, she wanted to spend some time with Mina, who would soon be graduating from university.

Some people argue that motorway tolls are high in France, but in my view their roads are the best in Europe and worth the extra expense. Even if we could ill afford it at the moment, more than anything I wanted the peace of mind that being on good roads afforded me. The rest stops in France are also very good for giving the dogs a run, with big, open, park-like areas. And while I was sorry Pascale wouldn't be travelling convoy with me, it was a comfort to me that at least she would be driving good roads much of the way.

Trying to get off to an early start never seems to work out for me – I always end up leaving a couple of hours or so later than planned. This trip was no different. I put Bush and Mitzi in the cab with me, and Altan, Tacki and Patchy went in the back. Once on the road, I made good time and got as far as thirty miles north of Lyon before stopping for the night. The next day, I was able to get off to a much earlier start and again was making good time until I got near the Mont Blanc tunnel. When we began to climb the long, sweeping ascent leading up towards the Alps, the poor old Renault started to heat up. I'd been pushing it, trying to make good time, so I eased off, using less throttle, and was glad to see the temperature gauge moving slowly back to the green. I knew if I pussyfooted my way as far as the tunnel, we'd be okay for the rest of the way, as it was all descent. My strategy slowed me up a lot, but I was able to keep going. At last I made it to the tunnel and passed through the French customs check at the entrance, then across the Italian side checkpoint, all without having to stop. Thinking back to how difficult crossing the border was in the seventies, the ease of crossing now only reinforced my opinion about the silliness of some rules and regulations.

Now that we were through the Mont Blanc tunnel and driving downhill, the Renault's engine was running cooler. I had lost a lot of time, though, and it was getting late so I found a place to stop for the night. I fed the dogs, took them for a run and went to bed. The next day I got up, eager to start the last leg of the journey. About thirty miles from Lake Garda and my turn-off to exit the autostrada, I heard a rhythmic "thump, thump" noise start somewhere in the back of the truck. It was worse when I applied the brakes. I stopped as soon as I could and checked the wheels, tyres, axle and everything else I could think of, but I couldn't find what the problem might be.

Continuing along the road, it got progressively worse. I stopped a couple more times to take a look but still couldn't find anything wrong. However, because there were just a few more miles to Antonio's house and the Renault kept going, I wasn't too worried. Approaching the exit ramp, I slowed down and steered to the right, following the curve, then back into a long, sweeping bend to the left as the road changed direction to go underneath the autostrada. As the inertia changed on the curve, the weight of the truck came down on the right-side suspension and I heard an even more pronounced "thump, thump, thump" – then a "bang" and the truck gave a jolt. I slowed down as quickly as possible and came to a stop at the side of the road. Looking in the mirror, I knew I had a major problem – the rear right wheel was sticking out at an angle!

I jumped down from the cab and hurried to the back for a closer look. I was horrified to see that all the bolts securing the double wheels had sheared. The inner wheel stayed on because the truck's weight was resting on the stubs of the bolts.

I don't know how I did it, but driving at a snail's pace I managed to make it completely off the autostrada exit, then stopped at the side of the road. I didn't dare risk driving any farther. If there was anything positive about this happening, it was its timing; a few minutes earlier I had been travelling at fifty-five miles an hour! I cringed at the thought – I could have had an accident with the dogs. Sizing up the situation, it was pretty obvious I couldn't fix it myself so I walked to an auto garage I saw in the distance. The mechanic was helpful and did a makeshift job, saying he would need additional parts for a more complete repair. This was just enough to get me to a more secure parking area.

I tried to phone Antonio. The line to his home was dead, so I phoned a cousin of his and left a message. Pascale had our mobile phone with her, so I called and told her what had happened. Because I'd been travelling much slower than her, she had nearly caught up to me.

"I should be with you in two or three hours," she said.

After taking the dogs for a run on the grass verge, I just sat there in the falling darkness, waiting for either Pascale or Antonio to show up. It was Antonio who came first. We greeted each other like brothers. I asked him, "Why couldn't I get you on the phone?"

"My father had the phone taken off. I got your message when I dropped in to see my cousin Luigi this afternoon."

I thought it a bit strange about the telephone, but strange things happening in Antonio's world were normal. When I told him about the gravity of the problem with the wheels, he kept grinning impishly which was disconcerting. But I forgave him; that was just his personality.

A while later, the Ford drove up and I was very pleased to have Pascale by my side again. She'd go to any length for the good of the animals and to keep the act in shape, but one thing she didn't like was to rough it in the tradition of circus life, preferring always to have the small luxuries such as being able to take a shower before going to bed. I had used up the reserve of water in the living trailer, so I expected Pascale to accept Antonio's offer to drive her on to the house for the night. However, she refused, preferring to forgo her luxury for one night and stay with me and the dogs.

The next day we had some hard decisions to make. The Renault would have to stay where it was until spare parts could be found. We decided to leave the vehicle on the outskirts of a town called Peschiera. We still had to find some means of getting the trailer, props and animals to Antonio's house. He returned to help and to show us the way to his house – we'd never yet been there or met any of his family.

We decided to risk towing the trailer with the Ford. Luckily, it had had a ball coupling for towing already installed when we bought it, although we'd never used it for pulling the trailer because it wasn't strong enough. We hooked the trailer to the car. Pascale rode in Antonio's car with Hansi, Mitzi and Tacki. I took Bush, Altan and Patchy with me, driving as slowly as I dared, yet not slow enough to be pulled over by the police for holding up traffic. We only had about twelve kilometres (eight miles) left to get to Antonio's house, but as we left the town behind, the road began to climb steeply and the engine, straining from the weight of the trailer, began to stall. In first gear, I had to play the revs of the engine against the spinning clutch and I nearly cooked it. I could smell the burning clutch and the acrid stinging odour made Bush sneeze. I felt sorry for that poor old Ford.

"Come on, old girl, you can do it," I said aloud.

Finally, we made it to the top of the hill. After passing through some more beautiful countryside, typical of that region, we turned into a driveway leading up to a big house. The driveway was lined with gorgeous pine, fig and olive trees on either side and led to an open space in the midst of a lush lawn. We stopped just short of the house and I let the dogs out and stood looking around. Everything seemed a little neglected, but even so, the splendour and beauty of the house and surrounding grounds couldn't be overlooked. It was early June and an abundance of trees and flowers were in full bloom. There was a complete absence of traffic noise. After the last three days on the road, this was heaven.

Antonio led us into the house to meet his parents. Mr and Mrs Marino were quite elderly – I thought possibly in their eighties and seventies, respectively. They welcomed us and immediately put me at ease over my doubts that maybe their son hadn't talked to them about us intruding into their lives like this. Later, Antonio took us out past a horse stable and continued down a short pathway until we arrived at a gate leading into a very picturesque meadow bordered by tall poplar trees.

"*Guardate Mike e Pascale, il vostro posto* – Look, Mike and Pascale, your place," he said. "We can put the trailer there and the truck next to it. Over there you have a tap to connect the trailer for water and here…" he pointed to a post next to the gate, "you have an electric plug. This meadow is all yours for as long as you like."

I didn't know how to thank him enough. This arrangement suited us perfectly. I looked at him and said, "*Grazie amico mio.*"

He just grinned back, then beckoned to us. He took us for a quick tour around the grounds. The house was built on one of the highest points of the lush, rolling countryside and the views were magnificent. It was in a winemaking region and there were vineyards with solitary manor houses standing in their midst as far as the eye could see, the red-tiled roofs glinting in the midday sunshine.

The Marinos' house was the most impressive of the manor-like houses. Built in the Tuscan style, it was three storeys high and must have had at least fifteen rooms including a huge dining room with the longest table I have ever seen. The side facing south had a covered porch that extended the whole length of the house. From there, we had a clear view over what Antonio told us were his father's vineyards. The porch had a step down to a sloping lawn in whose centre nestled an oblong swimming pool about forty-five feet long and thirty feet wide. Although it was empty and full of leaves, it otherwise looked in good condition.

Antonio could tell we were impressed and went on to explain that his father was a self-made man. Starting off with very little capital, he had built a meagre leather goods business into a huge factory, employing over a thousand people in its heyday. Antonio said his father had been in retirement for the last ten years and the factory was now standing derelict. I found that quite sad, but Antonio was still smiling.

After getting the trailer parked, Pascale got started tidying up, which had been neglected the past few days, while I took a couple of trips with the Ford back to the Renault to collect the props for the act and other necessities we hadn't had room for on the first run with the trailer. Our opening in the nightclub was in two days, which meant we had to rent a vehicle to get us there. That would just about use up the last of our money. However, our salary at the Schilling club would be five hundred thousand lire per day (two hundred and seventy English pounds), so I felt renting our transportation was a necessary expense that could easily be covered by our projected earnings. The Renault would have to stay where it was for a few days until we had the time and the money to get the repairs done properly.

*

The next morning Pascale found a car hire and put in an order for a light van for us to pick up the next morning. At lunchtime, Antonio came knocking on our door, saying his parents had invited us for a meal. We gladly accepted. The food they served us was delicious, and I felt humbled by their kindness. Hospitality ran in the family, so it seemed.

The next day we picked up the van, loaded the props in and got on the road for Modena. Usually when we go to work somewhere (except galas or TV shows), there is at least one day of rehearsals. When we worked in the amusement park in Germany, we had two weeks of rehearsals before the opening show. However, the arrangement with the Schilling called for a quick setup rehearsal for the lighting and sound at three-thirty in the afternoon, then perform the show at midnight.

We found the nightclub easily enough and arrived on time after an hour's drive. At the entrance, there was a glass case built into the wall displaying photographs of the striptease artists appearing in that evening's performance. They all had names like Miss Kitty, Barbara, Amanda and also more exotic names like "Pussy Amour". All the doors were locked and when we knocked, nobody answered, so we waited for somebody to show up. Eventually a man arrived and we introduced ourselves. He was courteous but very formal with us.

We followed him into the reception area, which had a small cloakroom, and I noticed how clean the establishment was. Then he led us through a door into what appeared to be the actual nightclub interior. The décor was all done in black with an occasional mirror. There were tables all around and a bit of floor space in the middle, but I couldn't see a stage or place for us to work. The room was well lit, and three men, whom I took to be waiters, were polishing the tables and mirrors with little white cloths. The man led us down some stairs at the far end of the room. I thought he was leading us to another part of the club where they put on the shows with the girls and whatever other acts they had engaged. But no, the stairs only led to the dressing rooms. My heart sank as it dawned on me – the little floor space in the middle between the tables was to be our stage. Pascale realised as well what was expected of us, and we both exchanged a look of disbelief.

I'm sure if Liliane had known, she wouldn't have sent us there in the first place, but obviously she hadn't been there to see for herself. If we'd had another three feet or so all round, I thought it might just be possible to work. But Bush needed at least a five-foot run after coming out of the trunk to have momentum enough to jump onto the cart, plus the width of the trunk, then the length of the cart, altogether requiring fourteen feet. The floor space was only about twelve feet square.

What I did realise rather quickly was that the nightclub owners were in complete ignorance of our difficulties. The act was offered to them by the agency, and they expected us to work under their conditions. Despite our misgivings, we decided to risk making complete fools of ourselves and try to do the act that night, improvising wherever we could and hoping it would go all right. We put the costumes in the dressing room and left the props in a corner. We had six hours to while away before getting back in time for the show.

There wasn't much money left, which lessened our options of what to do until showtime. We found a shady place under a tree near some public gardens where I could take the dogs for a run, then did our best to relax and prepare ourselves for later. The afternoon passed, and we went back to the club at eleven. Keeping Bush and Tacki with us, we went down to the dressing room to change and get ready. After putting on makeup and changing into my Bell Hop costume, I opened the door and stepped out of the dressing room to come face to face with Miss Kitty. I recognised her from the photographs outside. She was wearing a Stetson and cowboy boots and that's all. My jaw dropped open and I stared before reminding myself to act like a professional who's used to working in nightclubs. We said hello, then I continued on my way to prepare the props for the show.

The dressing-room area was alive with activity now. Some of the strip girls were even warming up as an acrobat does before performing. It triggered my fantasies as to what their routines might be. Most of them had costumes on, each one having a particular character to her look – Miss Kitty obviously used a Texas cowgirl theme and an Asian girl was dressed as a geisha. The thought struck me: what a lot of costume to get off in about six minutes! One of them even asked me to zip her dress up, which I took as an honour and sign of acceptance.

After the show got underway, one after another, the girls disappeared up the stairs in their costumes only to come back down again a few minutes later, nude and holding their costumes under their arms. When we brought the dogs out of the dressing room, the girls made a fuss over them. We spent a few minutes talking and joking with the girls before one of the waiters told us to be ready in five minutes.

Making our way with the dogs and props up the stairs wasn't easy, but with the help of a waiter I got everything into place. When our music began to play, I manoeuvred the cart between the tables, following Pascale onto the floor. For the men who enjoyed the mood created by the girls, we must have been a let-down for them. Looking back now, if we had had a fair chance and enough room to work properly, I think we would have been a big success, even with that audience. But it wasn't to be. Tacki did his best but didn't have enough space to do the rolls over my back. Bush misjudged his distances and kept missing tricks. Pascale and I couldn't use our movements and expression to sell the act to the audience as we normally do. Unfortunately, it was the disaster that I feared it would be.

The manager of the Schilling came to see us in the dressing room saying he had no option but to terminate our contract because the act wasn't what they expected. Anyway, he was kind enough to pay us the night's salary in full. If I could have seen any way of performing the act under the limitations of that setting, I would have tried to talk him into letting us stay on. I'm not a defeatist, but we just couldn't work there – it was no use. And I felt pretty bad in another way, too, because it was the first time in my life I'd been fired, or "given the sack", as we English say.

We could do nothing but pack up and leave, our figurative tails between our legs.

*

Arriving back at Antonio's in the chilly, early hours of the morning, even the splendour of our surroundings wasn't consolation to our demoralised spirits. The stark reality was that we had no work and hardly any money left.

We phoned Liliane later that day to explain what had happened. She apologised and said she'd try to find something else, but for the moment she had no other work available. We phoned other artistic agencies with the same negative result. Most of the summer season shows had already started, but those that hadn't opened yet were still fully booked for at least the next few months.

After arranging a loan to see us through until we could find work, we settled into a kind of routine at the Marinos' home. We phoned agencies daily and sometimes were invited to eat in the house (which helped Pascale's food budget). The dogs were having a wonderful time. I gave them long periods of exercise in the adjoining fields and vineyards.

Up until my stay at Antonio's, I never realised how much attention vineyards needed. During the daytime there at the house, people were pruning, watering and fussing around the vines all the time. Living in our own private campground near the big house and vineyards with the now-filled swimming pool at our disposal – all these luxurious surroundings taken in contrast with our imminent state of poverty made the situation seem unreal. Of course, we told Antonio what had happened with the Schilling. He told me if he could help in any way, he'd be only too pleased to do so. It seemed Antonio's sole purpose in life was to be of service to others and if everything wasn't a happy occasion, then it should be made into one.

The following days gave me more insight into the way of life at the Marinos' home. It turned out that Antonio's parents considered him to be the black sheep of the family. For some strange reason, this didn't surprise me. His father had wanted him to learn the family business and take it over when he retired, but Antonio hadn't been interested. In fact, he wasn't interested in much else either that could be of any use to his father. But that didn't mean he was lazy – it was more complicated than that. He lived life very intensely, driving back and forth between all the different people he knew. Also, his interest in horses occupied much of his time. To complete my description, Antonio saw a lot of a good-looking, sweet girl named Marcella.

I also noticed that Antonio was quite overbearing with his parents. To say they cowered from him would be a little exaggerated. Nevertheless, one day Mrs Marino took me into her confidence and told me that Antonio, from childhood, had been a difficult person where the family was concerned. Somehow, however, he had been easier on them since we'd come to stay and that was a big help to them. I was glad we were of some assistance to them other than just taking up room on their estate.

As far as I could tell, Antonio didn't work. I think he received an allowance from his father, but that didn't mean he lived a life of luxury. His car was a beat-up old Fiat and when we were out and about, he was always trying not to spend too much. But sometimes he did go wild. Once he invited Marcella, Pascale and me out to a fine restaurant and we had a splendid, expensive dinner together. The next day he was broke, but it didn't seem to bother him much.

*

Several weeks went by and we still had no luck finding work. It was as if the world of show business had forgotten us. It was hard for me to understand – one moment we were doing well-paid shows for TV and royalty, then nothing. The dry period after our Moroccan engagement hadn't been easy for us, to begin with – sometimes it had been months between contracts – so the disappointment at the Schilling nightclub hit us even harder. We were in a fragile financial state. Although we were telephoning agencies to try to find engagements, nothing turned up. I started to get depressed and began questioning what I did for a living. Pascale asked me if I thought perhaps I should go back to training horses. But I just couldn't imagine myself putting the dog act on the side to make room for horse training. I knew in my heart if we got the right breaks, the dog act would provide a commercially successful way of life for us. And on top of everything, I loved the dogs and never wanted to be parted from them; I never even wanted them to have to take second place to another act.

Sometime during the first two weeks' stay with Antonio, we managed to get new bolts fixed onto the wheels of the Renault and drove it to park alongside the trailer. Of course, the repairs had taken more of our much-needed cash. With the small loan I had arranged, we couldn't last much longer without money coming in. I arranged for another loan, knowing this would be the last – if that ran out before any jobs had turned up, we would be in a very difficult position. When we were working, even if it was irregularly, we could buy the basic necessities. But soon it would be a fight for survival. Something had to happen.

One of Antonio's favourite pastimes was driving around and stopping at the various cafés he knew. Travelling with him is how I became acquainted with the surrounding countryside. Lake Garda is a tourist region, with many picturesque villages and towns built onto the shoreline. Apart from wine, the tourist industry seemed to provide an important economic base for that area. Quite often, with nothing else to do, Antonio came knocking on the door of the trailer saying, "*Andiamo bere un caffè* – Let's go drink a coffee," and off we'd go. Most of the time I went alone with him, because Pascale was quite depressed about the work problem and preferred to stay at home. But one evening, Antonio suggested we travel to the nearby town some eight kilometres away. I was glad when Pascale agreed to come with us. It was the first time we'd been to this particular town, although it was one of the nearest.

If you look at a map, Peschiera is at the southern tip of Lake Garda, and as it broadens out, the town where we were going is a little farther down the coastline. Antonio's house was inland. So if you drew a line to connect those places, it forms a triangle.

The short run to town was very pleasant with the heat of the day replaced by a warm, soothing breeze coming through the open windows of the car. The smell of the trees and the fragrance of newly cut grass in the vineyards perfumed the air.

We parked the car and walked the short distance into the town centre. As with most Mediterranean cultures I'm familiar with, the towns in this area come alive at night. Throngs of people mill around, gracing everything with a festive mood. Antonio told us the population swelled by about eighty per cent at the peak of the tourist season. It was hard to believe that only five miles (eight kilometres) away was the calm and tranquillity of our meadow. I was glad to see Pascale laughing and joking with Antonio. It was good for her to get away from the trailer.

After walking along a busy narrow street where we often had to step off the kerb to pass other people, we found ourselves in a piazza with a lovely fountain in the centre. Beyond that was a harbour full of small yachts and sailing dinghies cheerfully bobbing and tugging at their mooring lines. The harbour formed a square that came into the middle of the town with just an outlet at the far end leading to the lake.

This part of town, closed to road traffic, had a wide walkway, or quay, extravagantly paved with marble that edged the harbour, stretching right to the water's edge and was bordered by cafés, restaurants and high-class gift shops. The shiny marble surface and the shimmering reflection of the lights on the water gave a rich, romantic air to this quaint setting. Most of the cafés had chairs and tables outside.

Antonio stopped in front of a café with a sign that said "Gino's" and beckoned us to follow him inside. When the young man behind the bar looked up and saw that grinning face, he cried out, "Hey, Antonio, long time no see!"

"*Ciao, Gino*," our friend responded, and proceeded to introduce us.

An old school friend of Antonio's, Gino had made good and, apart from being the owner of the café, was also a member of the town council. It always amazed me how popular Antonio was and how many people he knew. My original impression of him being a lonely person was wrong. We had a couple of drinks and when Antonio went to pay, Gino said the second round of drinks was on the house.

After we left the café, we continued along the walkway towards the lake. At the end we turned right and the marble paving gave way to a tarmac surface. There the walkway was even wider and I was surprised to see street artists working. Spaced about every ten metres, performers ranging from one person to groups of several people were plying their trade – jugglers, tarot-card readers, musicians and many other odd specialities. We continued walking along the quay and I noticed that some artists were more popular than others and attracted crowds so big one could hardly see what the performers were doing. Other acts drew only a few people. The artists thinned out towards the end of the quay, where the cafés gave way to hotels and private homes. We turned around and made our way back, stopping here and there along the way to watch the street show.

*

That evening out picked up our spirits a little, but as the days dragged on at the Marinos' home we found ourselves getting dramatically low on funds. We even found ourselves really looking forward to the times when we were invited to eat at the house. Almost daily at odd hours, and not necessarily including his parents, Antonio called us over and, playing host, cooked something simple for the three of us.

One thing I kept reminding myself of was not to neglect Altan's training. I couldn't get into the mood, though, afraid I'd do more harm than good if I tried – I had to be focused to do it properly. But I didn't neglect the dogs' wellbeing. Pascale and I always put the animals first and what little money we had left went first to dog and cat food. We could have given them scraps of leftovers, but that would really have been a last resort. I preferred to give them what they were used to: fresh meat cooked with rice or sometimes greenstuffs such as broccoli or cabbage mixed in. Through experience, I'd found that not only good food but the right amount was essential in keeping them healthy. I constantly examined them, feeling their sides to see how much fat they were carrying. Ideally, they should be fed well but not so much that you can't feel their ribs quite easily.

Sometimes, while dishing out the food for them and trying to get it just right, I've made their portions only one tablespoon different from the previous day's ration. One of my priorities was to keep the dogs healthy at all costs. Even if we didn't have work, we still had an act and should be ready to go to a job at any time.

Keeping ourselves psychologically positive was proving rather difficult, however, because apart from feeling depressed, a note of failure had crept into my thoughts. That in turn manifested itself in feelings of guilt and shame because of our reliance on the charity of the Marinos. Because I was brought up in class-conscious England, I thought maybe they would look down on us. But that wasn't the case. Sometimes after lunch Mr Marino asked me to stay for a while and over a cup of coffee he told me stories about his leather goods factory and times when he was younger. I found him a very likeable person and had nothing but admiration for him. One story stuck in my memory. It showed his very human side and depth of character.

When he began making leather goods, he went through a difficult time hardly selling enough to keep his family clothed and fed. Nearly destitute, he felt everything was against him; he was on the verge of giving up. Then he heard of a market that promised better sales. It was a long way for him to go and he didn't own a car, so he had to make the journey on a bicycle. In those days he only made one handbag at a time. He set off with the latest which was the best he had ever made. He actually sold it for a good price at the market and, with the money in his pocket, made his way home along the hot dusty road. About halfway there he saw an old man propped up against the railings of a bridge that spanned a river. Always ready to pass the time of day with someone, he slowed down. Getting nearer, he saw for the first time that the man had no arms and had a small cup in front of him, presumably for passers-by who could spare some change. Mr Marino found this strange, though, because the road was deserted. The man smiled up at him and gestured with the stumps of his arms and a nod of his head towards the cup. Mr Marino went on to tell me that a feeling of sympathy consumed him and, making a quick decision, gave the man all of his money – every last penny.

When Mr Marino got to this part of the story, he became very expressive, holding his two arms in front of him and saying, "I had my two arms – this poor man couldn't make anything even if he wanted to! My problems were nothing compared to his."

It was as if he suddenly had a vision of his life from a much broader perspective and rose out of any petty indulgences of self-pity he had been feeling. He made a vow then not to make one handbag at a time but hundreds.

So touched was he by this experience that he felt he had to make one last gesture of penance. Getting hold of the bicycle, he hurled it over the bridge into the river and walked the rest of the way home. Mr Marino told me that this almost religious experience changed his way of thinking and put him on the road to success.

Mr Marino's story gave me courage and strengthened my will not to give up but to persist; I felt sure our fortune was bound to change.

*

Our own plight made me wonder if Pascale and I were facing some kind of forced change in our lives. We still contacted the agencies as often as we could afford to. Because phoning with the mobile phone was expensive, we went to a local café and used the phone there. One Saturday a little over three weeks into our stay at the Marinos, Antonio drove me to the café to phone. The call to the agency sounded very promising and for the first time there seemed to be a genuine possibility of work for us in France. They asked me to call back on Monday, at which time they could tell me more about it.

Arriving back at the trailer, Pascale greeted me with a worried look on her face. Bush had vomited two or three times after eating his supper. Of course I was concerned and went to take a look at him. He wagged his tail when he saw me and didn't seem to be in any discomfort. It had been quite hot for some days, and I thought that was possibly the cause. The previous year while working in Gardaland, Bush had had a problem getting used to the heat and had vomited a few times. That time we took him to a vet by the name of Fedeli whom we knew from years before, when I had been with a circus in Verona. During the season we worked in Gardaland, the dogs had a few other minor ailments and Fedeli always made the right diagnosis and the dogs always responded to his treatment. This is why Pascale and I had utmost confidence in him where the dogs' health was concerned. Since arriving in Italy this time, we'd had no need of his services.

Fedeli's clinic, located in the centre of Verona, was an eighteen-mile drive from Antonio's. Additionally, it was past six o'clock and the clinic would certainly already be closed. This presented a dilemma, but I still didn't see Bush's vomiting as an emergency. I thought if I kept him off food and in a quiet, cool place, he'd be okay. I checked on him often, and around nine o'clock he vomited again, but this time it was only bile. This kind of thing happens sometimes with dogs when they eat grass to make themselves sick to clear out their stomachs. Apart from the vomiting, he seemed perfectly all right. I took him for a walk on the lead and he was very lively and wanted to play – he grabbed a stick in his mouth and jumped around. He was always high-strung, with lots of nervous energy. I tried to calm him down because I was aware of the life-threatening condition called torsion of the stomach that can be brought on by overexuberant exercise after eating. It afflicts mostly big dogs like Bush, but I didn't worry at the time that this was the problem, because one of the symptoms of this ailment is that the dog retches but can't vomit, and is in pain.

Bush was obviously not in any pain, but even so we decided to phone Fedeli and ask his opinion. At that hour, I knew it was no use phoning the clinic, so we found his home number in a telephone directory. But when we called, there was no answer. We made a place for Bush inside the Renault with all the windows open. It was getting cooler, and towards midnight he seemed to settle down, not having been sick again for some time. I stayed with him for a while, whispered a few soothing words, stroked his head and flanks, and said goodnight. In acknowledgement, he gave me a quick glance then lay his head down. Feeling quite exhausted myself, I joined Pascale in the trailer, had a shower and went to bed, thinking Bush would be okay by morning.

Sometime later I was jerked out of a fitful sleep by the sound of Bush vomiting again, and for a moment I just gazed into the darkness, listening. It was heartrending to hear him heaving and retching. I didn't want to wake Pascale unless there was a real emergency, so I eased myself out of bed and pulled on a pair of jeans and a T-shirt. Outside, I opened the door to the Renault and flicked on the light. Bush had finished throwing up and, calm once again, he looked up at me, blinking against the light with a sort of sad doggy grin and wagged his tail. His eyes were clear, which I took to be a good sign. I checked to see what he was throwing up and noticed it was a clear slimy liquid.

The weather was still quite warm, and I worried that he might be dehydrating. Dawn was just beginning to break and there was a misty dew hanging over the meadow when I took Bush outside for a walk. He started to run around, but I didn't want him to get too excited and restrained him on the lead. Back inside, I cleaned up the mess and enticed him to lie down and stay calm. He was panting and I began to worry again that he might be dehydrating and needed water. Fraught with indecision, I finally gave in to his obvious thirsty look and let him drink – maybe too much. It was a mistake that I'm still paying for with my conscience.

After drinking the water, Bush seemed to be all right. I was still with him when about twenty minutes later, he gave a convulsive shudder and a look of pain and fear clouded his normally happy expression. I knew something terrible was happening to him and, alerting Pascale, I ran to the house to get Antonio to help us find an emergency veterinary clinic that would be open at that hour. I knocked, then banged on the big double doors at the front of the house, but nobody answered. It was five-thirty and everyone was asleep. The bedrooms were at the back of the house and they couldn't hear me, so I ran round and, finding what I hoped was the window to Antonio's bedroom, I threw pebbles against it. After a third attempt, I saw Antonio's face grinning down at me.

"Please, we need your help, come quickly."

"*Arrivo subito*," he said.

We didn't have enough petrol in the Ford, so we used Antonio's car. I lifted Bush into the back. I can't remember most of the details of that ride to Verona; it was all so panicky. What I do remember is being in the back with Bush, holding him and trying to console him. He kept shifting himself about, which I'm sure was because of the pain. Pascale was sobbing, "Bush, oh, Bush." Antonio somehow got the address of a vet clinic, and knowing Verona so well, he knew how to get there without having to ask directions. When we arrived, I could feel Bush had swollen up as Pascale helped me lift him out of the car. After many years of experience in dealing with vets, we'd gained a kind of sixth sense as to whether they were good or not. We had a bad feeling about this one. He was young, probably just having passed his exams. He dithered about, giving the impression of being overwhelmed by the severity of Bush's illness. In a futile attempt to do something positive, Pascale said she'd drive with Antonio to Dr Fedeli's house to wake him and bring him here if necessary.

I was left alone with Bush and the poor vet who wanted to do all he could but was somehow incapable of taking any drastic action to save Bush's life. He told me it must be a torsion of the stomach and the only thing to do was operate, but he had never performed this procedure alone. I looked into Bush's eyes, and he didn't seem to be focusing anymore.

I felt distraught and helpless, and kept caressing him, saying, "Hang on, Bush, hang on." An indeterminate time passed, then I went outside to get some air. Outside, I paced as though I could hurry Pascale and Antonio back with Dr Fedeli. I had no sense of how long ago they'd left and looked up and down the road, hoping to see them arrive. I felt as long as there was a breath of life left in Bush, even if it was at the last moment, Dr Fedeli would save him.

Then I heard the door of the clinic open and close behind me. I turned round to face the vet in his white coat. He looked at me gravely and said, "*Mi dispiacce, e' morto* – I'm sorry, he's dead."

I rushed back inside. Bush was lying on the floor, his unseeing eyes already a glazed stare. I was overcome with grief, unable to come to terms with what had happened and not wanting to believe he was dead. And behind it was the faint, sickening awareness that my giving Bush the water had led to the fatal torsion of his stomach. It had all happened so quickly. No matter what I write, it cannot do justice to the horrible feelings of loss and remorse that overpowered me.

The vet left me alone with Bush and I sat on the floor next to him and talked to him, wanting to believe that somehow, on another plane, he could hear me. I thanked him for everything he'd done for us and told him how much I was going to miss him and how sorry I was. I knew that all my unashamed emotions would have to be expressed now, while I was alone with him, because later my feelings would be eclipsed by Pascale's grief and I'd have to support her in the coming days. A few years before, she'd made me promise that when we retired Bush, he'd be hers to spoil as much as she wanted. Now, Pascale would be denied his wonderful companionship.

Some minutes later, the mobile phone rang and I went outside to take the call. It was Pascale talking as fast as she could and almost tripping over her words. She explained they were at Dr Fedeli's, and he was willing to help and they were ready to leave. I could scarcely get a word in.

"Pascale, Pascale, Bush is dead."

There were a few seconds of silence, then the sound of her weeping. "No, no," she cried, over and over again.

We buried Bush two days later near some trees in a secluded part of the garden. For several days Pascale was inconsolable, then she sank into a heavy state of apathy and I could no longer communicate with her.

I too was very depressed. Before Bush's death, the act was still intact and we were just waiting for some gig to turn up; now we couldn't even accept work if it came. Was Bush like the bicycle in Mr Marino's story, a last gesture of penance? No, never – never the life of a trusted friend and partner like Bush. If I had the choice between success and him, I would choose Bush without a moment's hesitation.

Even so, we were at rock bottom – no work, no money and no act. As far as I could see, there was only one way left for us to go now, and that was up.

*

Collecting my thoughts, a kind of warrior spirit engulfed me, and an idea began to form. I looked at Altan, snapped on his lead, and took him for a walk. Finding some shade under a tree, I sat down and Altan lay next to me. I told him it was all up to him now, that Tacki would be his partner and would help carry him through. From now on he was to act like a pro.

Furthermore, I thought to myself, if work won't come to us, we'd go to the work.

Probably the most difficult period in training a new dog is starting to work him in live performances. Up until then, if he misses a trick, I can take my time and go back to it as often as I liked. But before an audience, that's not possible – it would spoil the act if I broke the rhythm of the storyline. So ideally, with a new dog, he is already doing the routine almost to perfection before I make the judgement of which is the right day for him to make his debut.

For most dogs, it's a surprise to find themselves in front of an audience. Others don't even seem to notice there's a difference from the training. Whichever way it goes, it's always a delicate phase while I make professionals out of them. One thing that helps is to keep using the principal dog, which in Altan's case would have been Bush. The new one then works only a couple of times a week and in between those days has training sessions, correcting anything that has gone wrong in the live performance. That way, he gets used to audiences gradually and I minimise the risk of my employer feeling he isn't getting his money's worth.

Awakening to the new situation and fortified by my decision to try something different to get us back on the showbiz circuit, I asked Antonio if it would be possible, with the help of his friend Gino, to get the necessary permit to work on the street. Always ready to help and pleased to have a reason to drive over to one of his haunts to see a buddy, he said "Let's go and see him now."

It was during the daytime when business was slack at Gino's so we had a good opportunity to talk to him. Gino said the rules stated that first, a permit had to be granted for the town of Verona before any of the other towns in the province would look at an application. However, he thought obtaining a permit for a dog act might prove to be difficult.

Anyway, we'd taken the first step, and the next morning Antonio and I drove to Verona. First we went to the town hall. They told us we should go to the tourist office. The tourist office sent us to the police station. The police station told us to go back to the town hall. Each time we had to wait in line to speak to someone in charge. It was five in the afternoon by the time we got back to the town hall and they were closing, so we had to call it a day with zero accomplished.

Next day, after I'd seen to the dogs, Antonio had breakfast with us in the trailer. The extra company helped lift Pascale's morale and, for the first time, she spoke about their ill-fated trip to Dr Fedeli's house. Ironically, when we decided not to phone his clinic because we thought it was closed, he was actually there doing an emergency operation on a big dog at the clinic for the same ailment that had afflicted Bush. That's why there was no answer at the house. Antonio and Pascale had arrived at Fedeli's house at about six-thirty, and he had just come home. Pascale told us that Fedeli had said that Bush, with his high-strung character, was the typical type of dog to suffer a torsion of the stomach – and that it was nearly always fatal.

That was little consolation to me, because I was sure I'd made the mistake of giving him too much to drink. Thankfully the conversation turned to a lighter subject, and we discussed my idea of working in the street. Pascale wasn't happy about it because of security issues for the dogs – that they would be vulnerable to accidents in such a busy area. I argued with her, saying that part of town was closed to traffic.

She said, "Okay, but what happens if a big, dangerous dog comes along?"

I had to admit she had a point, but I believed we'd get round that somehow, if and when the time came.

The truth was that, for all my so-called warrior spirit, I was hoping it wouldn't come to us having to actually work in the street. On one hand, my thought process went something like this: I can never go through with this; it would be demeaning and it would be like begging. The shame – what would my father have thought, my grandfather and grandmother, and Lord George? They would all be turning in their graves at the thought of one of the family offspring brought down to this.

On the other hand, I thought, I must go ahead; it is the only way to get us going again. I knew I had to move forward with the plan.

*

After coffee and toast, Antonio and I drove back to Verona. With him, it was compulsory to stop at a café along the way. I wanted to keep moving to get things done, but with him you had to give and take on issues like that. He liked going into the cafés to socialise, not because he wanted something to drink. After ordering two coffees, he got into a conversation with some men standing at the bar drinking cappuccinos. After I'd finished my coffee, I became impatient. "*Scusi signori, possiamo andare Antonio?* – Excuse me, gentlemen, can we go, Antonio?"

Sometimes I wished he would take life more seriously. But, on the other hand, while I was more uptight and focused on the situation, Antonio's happy-go-lucky attitude helped me see a lighter side and balanced our relationship. I really was grateful to have him helping me.

On arriving in Verona, we went to the town hall. There, we learned the duties of the tourist office where we'd gone the day before were to help tourists with their questions, but official business had to be dealt with here in the town hall.

The size of the town hall corresponded to the size of Verona – it was a big rambling building with a wide staircase in the centre going up four levels. Each level had numerous doors bearing signs announcing that department's function. We finally found a door with "UFFICIO TOURISTICO" written on it. Antonio knocked and I followed him inside. It was a big room with a wide wooden counter that ran the length of one side. A long line of people almost hid two ladies standing behind the counter answering questions and handing out forms. Eventually it was our turn and the younger woman called, "Next, please."

Antonio fixed her with his smile. She returned his smile and cocking her head to one side, gave a silent, "Well, what can I do for you?" look.

Typically, wanting to add some drama, Antonio hesitated, then, widening his smile, he said, "*Buongiorno, Signorina.*" Antonio was charming her, so I let him do most of the talking. She seemed quite nice and the conversation progressed on a positive note until the dogs were mentioned. She shook her head, no, and said she didn't think they'd let a dog act work in the street. For all Antonio's charm, this wasn't going well; it was time for me to say something. In as few words as possible, I told her my story of bad luck since arriving in Italy, stressing that I didn't have any money left and working in the street would be my only salvation.

My direct and sincere way of talking was having an effect because she wasn't saying no any longer. She asked me a lot of questions, such as how much room I needed and whether the dogs were well behaved and not likely to bite someone. Then she asked if I had any descriptive literature of the act. I'd come prepared and handed her some photographs and souvenir programmes of shows we'd done. Taking them, she said she'd show them to the head of her department and asked us to come back the next day.

Before leaving, Antonio asked her name.

"Lydia," she said with a smile.

Well, our path to working in the street wasn't proving easy, but I was determined at least to get the permission.

The next day we set off for Verona again. First we made the customary stop at a café, then we arrived back at the town hall. Lydia said her superior was sympathetic to my application, but they wanted assurance the act would be presented in a professional manner. They needed a signed paper from an artistic agency saying I was authentic. I thought this a bit strict just to work in the street, but I was overjoyed with the positive attitude of the tourist office people. I'd do whatever they wanted.

I phoned the Tavel agency in Paris, which had arranged for us to work the gala show for King Hassan II, and asked them to write a simple note of verification on their letterhead. To save time, I asked them to fax it straight to the tourist office. While waiting for it to arrive, Antonio, of course, suggested going to a café. When we got back, we had to wait in line again. Finally, when it was our turn, Lydia told us they received the fax and it would take some time to process everything. She asked us to come back in two days.

Two days free of having to drive around would give me more time to concentrate on Altan's training. I knew I had to spend as much time as possible getting him ready to work in the street. He still wasn't doing the last two tricks of the act.

I should have felt tired mentally, if not physically, with all the driving around with Antonio and worry about whether everything would work out. But the fear of losing the way of life I loved – working with the dogs, travelling the world, putting on performances and show business in general – kept me going. If I had the guts to work in the street, then nothing after that would ever worry me again.

The next day was very hot and in the first training session just before midday, Altan was very sluggish and things didn't go so well. I used a makeshift dummy of myself standing on my head. It was quite crude, but it did the job of giving Alton a life-like image. I would use that until he was far enough advanced with me helping him, then I'd take its place in the final stages of learning the trick.

After our last training session, just as the sun was setting, I visited Bush's grave and stood quietly under the trees, cherishing this time with him. I knew that sometime, inevitably, we'd have to move on and I wouldn't be able to come here anymore. Also, looking down on that small mound of earth, I needed this physical confirmation of his death. Only a few days before he was in the best of health and part of our lives.

Over the years, the death of our dogs had been my only direct confrontation of death and I started to question what comes after. No easy answers came, but I had to believe our loved ones somehow stay connected to us for eternity.

It was getting dark and I still had the dogs to see to, so I made my way back to the trailer. Later, Antonio and Marcella came with a bottle of wine from Mr Marino's cellar, and we drank and talked until weariness got the better of us all. Before bidding us goodnight, Antonio said his father wanted to invite us to a party he was giving next weekend for some old friends and business acquaintances. "And don't forget, tomorrow we have to go back to the town hall in Verona," he said on parting.

Before going to bed I decided to change my plan with Altan and put aside training him on other tricks until the end trick had been accomplished. If we were soon to be working in the street, it would make more sense to have a good finishing trick ready for the audience. Even though I was tired, sleep didn't come easily. I was unable to silence the question running through my mind: would we get the permit tomorrow? According to Gino, if we couldn't get the permit for Verona, we couldn't work elsewhere in the region, either. But we had to make money somehow – and soon. Eventually I fell into an uneasy sleep.

The next morning, I got in a quick training session with Altan. I wasn't expecting any breakthroughs with him yet, and it went more or less like the previous day, just walking him through the trunk sequence of the act.

Antonio and I left for Verona and upon arriving we found a parking slot not too far from the town hall. When we eventually saw Lydia, she asked us to come back at two-thirty, adding that the permit should be ready by then. Naturally, I was overjoyed, but strangely, I also experienced an anxious feeling akin to stage fright at the thought of working in the street.

Walking out into the hustle-bustle of the town, I looked around, trying to imagine working the act out in the open. It stirred conflicting feelings of both dread and excitement. We found a café and Antonio ordered drinks and sandwiches for the two of us. He insisted on paying and I didn't argue. On the way back to the town hall we passed a flower shop and on what seemed to be a sudden impulse, my smiling friend disappeared inside. I followed him and waited patiently while he ordered two beautiful bouquets of red roses.

"What are you doing?" I asked.

"For Lydia," he said, thrusting one of the bouquets into my arms.

"But why two?"

"Yours is for Lydia, mine is for the other girl working in the office. We must not forget her," he said emphatically.

I felt a bit stupid standing in line at the tourist office with the flowers, but Antonio insisted this was the way to do it. I'm not sure who was more embarrassed when I handed them over to Lydia and thanked her for her efforts on my behalf.

The permit was an impressive-looking document, conspicuous by its stamps and signatures; it brought back memories of the red tape and bureaucracy I'd encountered when I tried to get Barny across the border. Lydia also handed me another piece of paper, explaining that it listed all the places we were not allowed to work. The paper contained a map of Verona, with specific parts marked with a red margin. They were mainly cultural tourist attractions including the world-famous arena where open-air operas were staged. Also out of bounds were areas where municipal buildings were situated. After further inspection of the document, I realised we could work almost anywhere in Verona *except* for tourist areas! So, in actual fact, the real reason for working in the street – to earn money – was almost entirely defeated. Tourists were out to have a good time and spend money, but the areas where we were allowed to work would be around city-folk going about their business who wouldn't be inclined to stop to look at some impromptu performance, let alone pay for the privilege. It was hard to imagine why the city employed such reverse logic with regard to its street artists.

Still, on the way home I felt elated, knowing I didn't have to wait in line at the stuffy town hall anymore. I looked forward to getting the permission from our town, which I thought should be easy now.

Again, with Antonio to help me, we set off a couple of days later to submit our permit application. The process was a little different from Verona because this town had one designated place along the quay that was a fixed event, making it one of the main tourist attractions for the town. Thus the application procedure was more practised and arguably allowed a more straightforward and professional way for artists to acquire work permits than we'd experienced in Verona. The first thing we had to do was to fill out a form, giving name, address, what we did and how much room was needed. There was no interview or any discussion; all we had to do was hand in the form and wait for them to contact us.

*

While we were driving back the short distance to the house, Antonio spoke up. "You know the party my father is giving on Saturday? He wanted me to ask if you would perform for the guests with your act."

The request took me by surprise and I paused before answering. Was Altan ready? I pushed the negatives aside – it would be a perfect dress rehearsal for working in the street.

"Sure, that's a good idea," I said. The prospect stirred my imagination and I felt genuinely excited about it. "The best place to do it will be on the lawn leading down to the swimming pool – if that's okay with your father."

"I'm sure it will be," he responded.

Now I had something definite to aim for. This would be Altan's debut.

On Saturday morning while out running the dogs, I noticed a party-catering truck parked outside the house. It looked as if this was going to be quite some party. Later on, I took Altan for a training session. That afternoon, Pascale said she didn't feel up to working in the act that evening and would I mind doing the routine on my own with the dogs? She'd made some improvement and I could communicate with her again, but she still withdrew when anything reminded her of Bush. I respected her wishes. Doing the act without Bush would hurt too much at the moment. I missed him as well, but it wasn't fair to dwell on Bush and at the same time expect Altan to do his best. Dogs have an uncanny way of knowing when my concentration isn't wholly on them and they take it personally. It actually weakens my bond with them. All my thoughts were now on Altan. If we were to have a future with the act, everything hung on his and my capacity to make him into a performer.

Guests would be arriving at 7:30pm, when cocktails would be served to start off the evening. We decided the best time to do the act would be about 8:30, before dinner. Antonio and I inspected the lawn; it had a slight slope. After choosing the flattest part, we started setting up the props. I was starting to feel butterflies in my stomach at the thought of performing. It was strange, because I've done prime-time TV shows, worked in circus shows seating thousands of people, and here I was getting stage fright at the thought of working in front of a relatively small crowd.

One of the nice things about Italy is the weather – it is predictably warm and fair. It was a fine evening and ideal for working outside. Mr Marino called us over to meet his guests. True to his character, he treated us with respect, having no qualms at introducing us to everybody. Still, I couldn't shake my sense of failure. I felt inferior amongst these people, whom I thought must in the majority be accomplished businesspeople.

While Pascale and Antonio lingered on, chatting with Mrs Marino and a group of guests, I withdrew into a corner. Antonio saw me go and followed me. A few minutes later Pascale also joined us. I wasn't surprised that Antonio preferred our company to the other guests. I knew him well enough by then to realise he shunned anything to do with the family business or ex-associates of his father.

We were offered drinks. Pascale and Antonio accepted, but I demurred – I never drink before working. I was, however, looking forward to a glass or two afterwards when, hopefully, we'd have something to celebrate. Antonio could hardly contain his excitement and said, "Isn't it time to bring the dogs over?" He finished his sentence with a childish giggle. I found it quite comical to see him display this nervous anticipation at our performance.

But his happiness at being involved with the act was infectious and Pascale was just as amused as I was at Antonio's mood. We smiled at each other, then she took my hand for an instant. In the warmth of her smile and the touch of her hand for the first time since Bush's death, I again felt the loving bond between us. It was always there, but her open affection towards me had been dulled by our recent troubles and the torment of Bush dying. We had lost our usual communication and openness towards each other and I even believed it was hurting our relationship to the point that we had crossed some invisible line and might never be the same together. I realised at that moment that I had been filling the void of her affection with work. I'd been working as hard as I could to get everything done, like chasing after the permit and getting Altan ready, but now as I looked into her eyes, I knew how much I had missed and secretly craved her open affection. For that instant our eyes lingered on each other, it was as if everything that had been left unsaid was now said. I knew everything would be all right, that our love for each other would stand this trial of hard times.

"It's eight-fifteen," Pascale said between sips of her drink. "Don't you think it's time to fetch Altan and Tacki?"

"All right," I said, "let's get this show on the road."

Leaving her and Antonio to get the props into position, I hurried to the trailer where Altan lay in front of the door, tied up on a long lead, oblivious to the fact that he was about to work in front of an audience for the first time. When he saw me coming, he looked up sharply. "Isn't it time to feed me?" his expression asked, as I bent down to unhook the lead. Feeding time was overdue, but I couldn't give him anything before working. What he didn't know was that Pascale had prepared a nice surprise of chicken and rice for him for later.

Working with dogs like Bush who have been doing the act for a long time was easy insofar as they are more professional and do everything in a routine fashion. Younger dogs, on the other hand, are much livelier, which makes working with them exciting. I could see Altan wouldn't be an exception. He started jumping around as I tried to get the lead on him. I left Tacki with Pascale and, trying not to show my nervousness – which could disturb his mood – I started to prepare Altan.

Of course, it needed to be a surprise for the audience when he came out of the trunk, so I made sure we were out of view from the ongoing party before putting him inside. Patting him, I said a few "good boys" to encourage him, and closed the lid. With Antonio on one end and me on the other, we carried the trunk into position. Mr Marino gave a short announcement for the guests to assemble and ushered them into a group farther up the sloping lawn towards the house. Then Pascale gave a signal for someone to push the start button on the CD player and the dog act music burst into life from two conveniently placed loudspeakers. I took hold of the handcart with the luggage on it and made my way onto our makeshift arena.

Spurred on by Mr Marino's loud clapping, the guests started to applaud my entrance, and as I manoeuvred past the trunk I whispered to Altan one more "good boy". Positioning the cart in line with the trunk, I unloaded the luggage and with my back to the trunk, I put one foot on the left handle of the cart. Then I gave Altan the cue for him to come out of the trunk and jump up onto the other end of the cart. This first time for Altan in front of an audience, it was imperative that I exaggerate the cues to be sure to catch his attention. I clapped loudly and at the same time called out sharply, "*Altan*." It worked. He pushed the lid up with his head, leapt out and, with one bound, shot up onto the high end of the cart, sending his end down and my end up with all the force of his seventy-five pounds. Because I was paying so much attention to getting Altan to do his part, I had positioned myself too far forward over the stainless-steel handle. Instead of the handle stopping just short, it hit me like a sledgehammer in the crotch.

"*Ouch!*" I doubled over in pain, but hearing the laughter and applause of the guests, I somehow overcame the feeling that I'd been castrated and carried on. In the far corner of my mind that kept track of such things, I made a mental note that my real pain had shown me a better way of selling that trick and in the future, I would act it out more vigorously.

I turned round and was relieved to see that Altan, true to his training, had disappeared back into the trunk. I pushed the cart out of the way and started stacking the suitcases. I placed one of them end up and turned to get the next one. Altan performed his part perfectly; he jumped out of the trunk, pushed it down and was back inside before I turned back again. He was working well and we were getting a good response from the public. Sometimes he'd stop in the middle of a trick and gape for a moment at all the people, but their presence, if anything, just interested him as opposed to making him nervous. I still had to make the commands very clear, which spoiled the surprise effect of the unfolding story, but that didn't matter so much. The important thing was that Altan was doing everything I asked, and I was proud of him.

After completing the last trick, I called him to me and we took a bow, finishing the performance.

The act, of course, wasn't up to its normal standard of professionalism, but the guests seemed happy with the evening's surprise entertainment. I hugged Altan and Tacki, fussing over them and showering them with exclamations of "good boy", leaving them no doubt they'd done well. Then I took them back to the trailer and gave them their well-earned supper.

I was still hurting from my encounter with the cart handle, but that wouldn't stop me from celebrating Altan's debut. I went back to the house and joined Pascale and Antonio for a drink. Antonio was grinning from ear to ear and, as Pascale looked on with a sheepish smile, he thrust his arms out in front of him, holding a hat full of money. I looked down in disbelief and astonishment. It wasn't my intention for the hat to be passed, and I felt embarrassed. But Antonio said it had been his father's idea.

When I looked at the money again, I saw, amongst lesser denominations, a crispy one hundred thousand lire note (about fifty-five pounds) standing out boldly on its own. Looking up, I saw Mr Marino smiling benevolently at me across the crowded room.

*

The money we received that evening was only a third of what we would have earned in one day at the Schilling nightclub. But it was still a very welcome respite to our dwindling financial reserves. The next day Pascale was able to do some shopping for little necessities other than food.

While waiting for permission to work in town, I thought we might benefit from a rehearsal in the street. The town of Verona was a logical choice. Pascale wasn't keen on going into such a big city, but Antonio made up for her reluctance, bolstering my confidence with his exuberant enthusiasm.

"*Andiamo Pascale*," he said, and proceeded to gently talk her into accepting my idea. In preparation, I needed to practise getting the props into position and wanted us – both the dogs and me – to get the general feel of working in that kind of environment.

Finally, a few days after the party, we managed to load everything into the Ford by flattening the seats in the back. The rear door that swung upwards wouldn't close completely, so I had to tie it down, pulling it tight against the prop trunk, which was sticking out. The dogs love riding in cars, and when I opened the front passenger door, Altan and Tacki jumped onto the seat, their tails wagging. Pascale rode in Antonio's car, following me, and off we went. By the time we arrived in Verona, it was late afternoon. I drove around looking for the perfect place, preferably with not so many people. Psychologically, I was struggling with the begging part. I felt like a coward, but I wanted to introduce myself slowly to this new way of working.

Antonio and Pascale were patient and followed me around for half an hour. Finally, they overtook me and stopped in front of me. I drove up alongside them.

"What are you doing?" Pascale called through the open window.

I felt a bit flustered, knowing deep down I was just stalling.

I said, "Okay, I promise the next likely place I see I'll stop."

After driving round for another ten minutes I was ready to give up and headed out of town towards home. Just inside the city limits I saw a deserted-looking church with a large parking area in front, so I pulled over and stopped. *Yes*, I thought, *that should serve our purpose.*

Verona was dotted with churches everywhere. Large ones, small ones, some in good repair, some not. This one looked derelict. The heavy wooden front doors had battens nailed across them in a haphazard fashion. Bits of masonry were missing from its structure, which added to its overall impression of being abandoned. It was a once majestic but now dilapidated monument to an era of religious fervour. Few people were in sight, maybe because it was the evening mealtime, which suited me just fine. The sun was sinking behind the surrounding high-rise apartments and the overall hustle-bustle of the day was winding down.

We unloaded the props, first laying down a large piece of carpet to prevent the dogs injuring their paws on the bare concrete and also to protect the leather cases from getting scratched. We must have made an unusual sight in this quiet neighbourhood. A couple strolling with two small children who were eating ice cream walked in our direction and stopped a few yards away.

"*Ma, che cosa fanno loro, papa? –* What are they doing, Dad?" The smaller child looked up at the man holding his hand, expecting an answer.

"We are going to put on a show," I answered for him.

"*Bene –* Good," the man said with a smile.

I wanted this to be a happy experience for the dogs, so to prepare them I called them to me. Altan jumped up at me, I fell over backwards, and we rolled around on the carpet with Tacki trying his best to join in the fun. This went on for a few minutes and when I looked up, an old man and a teenager on a bike had joined our company of spectators. *It's now or never*, I thought.

We were in full view of everybody as I lifted the trunk lid and coaxed Altan to jump inside. The element of surprise would be missing when he came out, but that couldn't be helped. While I was doing that, I saw Antonio pull a cap from his trouser pocket. He threw it down in front of the onlookers. I was sure his timing of doing it at the last moment was to avoid me protesting.

I pretended not to notice and began the act. There was laughter mixed with "oohs" and "aahs", and the children giggling when I fell over the cases that Altan overturned. As the routine progressed, whenever Altan made a mistake, I did the trick again until he got it right. I discovered this kind of impromptu audience was more tolerant and open to improvisation than if they had to pay for a seat to see a show. The most positive aspect of doing the show this way, however, was something I'd never been able to do before with a new dog. I could treat this as a rehearsal and at the same time get Altan used to an audience.

At the end I took a bow, and the crowd of onlookers applauded. The cap had its provocative effect, and contributions came from the family with the kids, the old man and another couple who had joined the crowd. As the people began to disperse, Antonio scooped the cap up and peered inside. There were two five thousand lire notes and two thousand lire in coins. Antonio and I grinned at each other. Twelve thousand lire – seven pounds. *Not bad*, I thought, and praised Altan and Tacki with lots of "good boys" and hugs.

"I didn't expect anybody to give anything," Pascale commented drily.

"Well, you see, it might be worthwhile to work in the street," I said.

Antonio was even more animated than usual. "Let's go drink a coffee somewhere."

For once, I was enthusiastic about his expected proposition – actually, I thought this was a *very* appropriate way to finish this successful first afternoon as a street performer!

*

In the days that followed, I gradually grew more confident, although I was still hoping some miracle would happen that would spare us from working in the street. Even though it was my idea and I felt we had no other option, I still viewed it as something beneath the dignity of the act. To overcome those negative thoughts, I had to believe it would lead us to better things, and that's what kept me going.

In the meantime, Altan's training was making slow progress. We were stuck on the part after Altan pushes me into the trunk. The next step is for him to go round and push the lid closed. The problem in training this part was, if I did the sequence of the trick as it would be done in the show, I'd be in the trunk and unable to lead him through the rest of the trick, which was, after pushing the lid closed, running around and putting his paws on the front end to simulate pushing the trunk away while I was inside.

I'd trained him to run up to me from behind and push me. That part was going okay, and he could do it without any guidance from me, but I had to lead him through the rest of the sequence. This had gone on for some time, and we should have been at the stage where he knew what to do on his own, but every time I let myself fall into the trunk, he was at a loss as to what to do next, and because I was in the trunk, I couldn't help him. The only thing to do was to have patience until he understood what I wanted.

We were still waiting for the local permit. I spoke to Antonio about it.

"Maybe Gino can help move things along," he said. "Let's go and see him."

We drove down into town and found Gino. He was pleased to see both of us, and greeted me like an old friend. We explained our concern about the permit taking such a long time.

"That's not my department," he said, "but I will do what I can."

While Antonio and I ordered two beers, we could hear Gino on the phone. A few minutes later he walked over to our table.

"I just called Mr Antonioni. He is on the committee for tourist events. He said there is a holdup on your application because two of the committee members wanted to be reassured as to how the dogs would behave." Gino went on to say there would be a meeting tomorrow and he would do his best to sway the vote for us. We thanked Gino for his help and Antonio ordered two more beers.

It was late afternoon the next day when Gino called.

"It wasn't easy to convince them, but the tourist committee members are willing to give you a chance. They will issue you a permit to work in the street on a trial basis. If there are any complaints about the dogs, it will be revoked." He also said it was lucky we came to him for help because the application had been shelved because of the controversy and wasn't on the agenda anymore. His intervention had gotten things moving again. I thanked Gino and told him we'd do the act in front of his café, if he wished.

Gino laughed and said, "Okay, it's a deal."

We picked up the permit the next day at the town hall and set about making plans for our local debut. The permit indicated we were allowed to work between eight and eleven-thirty in the evening any day of the week up until the middle of September. It was now the middle of July.

That evening we went into town to find a suitable spot to work. The only place still free was at the end of the quay where the cafés started to give way to hotels and private homes. The crowds were thinner there, but that kind of satisfied my not wanting to make too much fuss about this working in the street business. As far as I was concerned, the quieter the better, for the moment anyway.

The next morning, I put Altan and Tacki through a training session. In the afternoon I loaded the props into the Ford, squeezing everything in as I'd done on our trip to Verona. We waited until seven-thirty in the evening, then, with Pascale riding in Antonio's car, we drove to town. We were able to park quite close to the spot where we wanted to work. I left the dogs in the car with the windows open, and in a few minutes the three of us working together had the carpet spread out and props set up. There were few people at our end of the quay when we arrived. It was still early and I suspected most of the tourists in town were still enjoying their evening meal. We decided to wait a while before doing the act. I put the leads on Altan and Tacki and walked them around for a while, getting them used to this new environment.

When I started playing with them on the carpet, the same thing happened as when we worked in front of the church. The few people who were nearby became curious about this new attraction. I was terribly nervous, but after counting fifteen people waiting for something to happen, I went ahead and did the act. As we progressed into the routine, the audience's laughter and applause helped me gain confidence. It also drew the attention of passers-by, and the original crowd had grown to at least double by the time we concluded.

After we finished, Pascale and Antonio went round with the hat, thankfully sparing me that awful job. I did my part by taking care of the dogs. We did the act once more that evening and earned about sixty thousand lire, or thirty-three pounds for the night. Pascale was happy at the prospect of going shopping the next day. And Altan was getting more comfortable with an audience, which made me happy. Amazingly, as I became able to control my initial nervousness, I found I enjoyed myself. It was actually fun!

*

The next day I found a square piece of plywood, and after sandpapering and varnishing it, I painted on it in bright red letters, "THE SANGERS" and "NEXT SHOW". Underneath, I left a space to write in chalk the time of the next performance. Finally, I screwed a bracket to the back so it would stand up on its own. That evening when we drove to town, not being tied down to a contract, I felt a kind of freedom in being able to choose our schedule for doing the act.

After laying the carpet down and getting the props into place, I wrote "8:30" on the board. Sure enough, twenty minutes past eight people started to gather, forming a circle round our setup. I fetched the dogs from the car. Altan pulled against the lead, eager to get going. With no music and Pascale absent from the routine (she preferred to be on the lookout for dangerous dogs), I felt rather strange, but I wanted to build that feeling into something positive, and instead of subduing it I absorbed it as a new experience.

During the three times we worked that evening, whenever I felt Altan needed to be reminded his work was a fun thing, I'd stop the routine to play and fool around with him. This helped even more than I could have imagined to develop his character in a way that suited the act – more than it had with any of the other dogs I'd previously trained. The viewing public took it as part of the act to see me play with the dogs and showed their approval. And something else occurred that I could never have foreseen: the close proximity of the public was helping me develop as an artist, for I began to interact with them, using dialogue. (Sometimes they got too close and Pascale or Antonio had to move them back.)

Once, as I was preparing Altan for a trick, he kept turning his head away towards a dog barking in the distance. I called his name a number of times, trying to draw his attention, but he wouldn't listen. In frustration, I had a spontaneous idea and barked like a dog. Altan looked at me, surprise in his eyes. I definitely got his attention – and a tremendous laugh from the public! That kind of casual ad-libbing had the effect of bridging the gap between me and the audience.

As I became more experienced at working in the street, this interaction with the audience took me to new levels, and I began to feel as one with them. I realised it was something that had been missing from the way I worked. The prowess of the dogs had always been the strong point of the act. Now I was able to be on a par with them. By doing this, I was complementing and enhancing the overall impact of the act.

We settled into a routine of working three to four days a week. I used the off days to practise the two missing tricks. Then, one such training day, bingo! Altan pushed me into the trunk then ran round the side, pushed the lid closed and, putting his front paws on the opposite end of the trunk, completed the whole sequence of the trick without any assistance from me.

The next day in town, ad-libbing, I said, "*Signore e Signori*, Altan will now perform this next trick for the very first time in front of an audience."

There was a spontaneous round of encouraging applause.

"Are you ready, Altan?" I said, taking my position in front of the trunk with my back to him. I waited a few moments to build up the suspense (a drum roll would have been appropriate). One could sense the anticipation as a hush fell over the spectators. I clapped my hands as a cue for Altan to run up and push me into the trunk. He did and carried on to finish the rest, all on his own. There was a sense of relief and rapturous applause from the crowd, as Altan seemingly pushed the trunk along with me bundled up inside. At last we had a fitting finale for the act. I was so proud and pleased with Altan that I hugged and praised him more effusively than usual – so much so that Tacki became jealous and would have started a fight with Altan if I hadn't quickly included him in my affections.

I did the same introduction of a new trick about a week later, after Altan learned to do the part where he jumped through my legs. "Ladies and gentlemen," I said, "Altan will now perform a new trick never before seen in public." Again, there was rapturous applause from the audience as he flawlessly completed the leg-jumping sequence.

At last the act was complete. Altan had surpassed all my expectations. He was getting more and more proficient. Slowly, I could do away with giving such obvious cues for him to do his tricks; the actual timing and sequence became the cues. As an example, he understood that when I positioned myself in front of the trunk, it was the moment to run and push me inside – so it was the moments and actions leading up to each trick that gave him the cue. With that accomplished, the act became fluid and more professional. Also, we were becoming the biggest attraction on the strip. One evening, in between our performances, we had a drink and a bite to eat in one of the nearby cafés. When we asked for the bill, the proprietor himself came to our table.

"No, it's on the house," he said. "I love to watch the dogs performing, and it's good for business. Usually, there are not so many people this far up on the quay. Your show has changed that."

We felt happy to have improved his livelihood – and to get a free meal, as well!

*

One day while working in own, Antonio showed me a newspaper article titled, "Centenary, Rastelli". It went on say that the city of Bergamo, with the participation of the Rastelli family, was to sponsor a circus festival honouring the world's most famous juggler, Enrico Rastelli, born there one hundred years before. Bergamo is an important northern Italian town about two hours' drive from Mr Marino's home. Rastelli's life played a prominent role in the town's history. I had worked with Rastelli's descendants just before I met Pascale. They had diversified from Enrico's juggling fame to become an acclaimed musical clown troupe that had worked in many well-known venues including the famous "Holiday on Ice" productions.

I was gaining confidence in Altan's ability and thought there might be a chance for us to work in that festival. I no longer had contact with the Rastellis, so I phoned an Italian agent by the name of Pino for whom we had worked on occasion. I asked him to try to negotiate the work for us. Two days later Pino called to say he'd been in touch with the Rastelli family and they remembered my act. He went on to tell me their budget for the festival was almost used up, but if I didn't expect a high salary, they could fit us in. At that moment I didn't care how much we'd earn for the act, I just wanted to get going again, so I worked out a salary that Pino thought would be acceptable. A few days later, we received the contract; we had to be there in two weeks to start rehearsals!

That evening, after giving our last performance in town, a few of Antonio's friends, including Marcella, joined us at our favourite café. "This is to toast the signing of Altan's first contract," I said, raising my glass of wine.

Altan was lying beneath our table. He raised his head when he heard his name. I reached down and caressed his flank, giving him my usual praise – "Good boy!"

To give ourselves time to clean up the props and do minor repairs, we decided to quit working in the street two days before leaving for Bergamo. For me it was an emotional affair. I felt I was leaving a piece of our lives on that little patch of tarmac next to the water's edge. So many things had changed in that short time. Working in the street had given me the freedom to experiment with my own performance and the way in which I trained Altan. He had become a professional faster than any of my previous dogs, cutting the usual two years of training by six months. And what a pro he'd become! When he worked, it was with a particular aura and charm that endeared him to the audience. I'm grateful my methods helped him develop and gave him the freedom to acquire his unique style.

And I'd also changed for the better; I bridged that gap to the audience. All these years I'd struggled to find a way, but until I began to work on the street, I'd been unable to do it. It's a little hard to define, but I think it was the close proximity to the audience that allowed me to open myself to them, and in turn they had done likewise, creating a friendly atmosphere where even mistakes in our work were taken in good humour. I gained an acceptance I had never experienced before. I couldn't wait to put the new zest the act had acquired to the test in a circus ring before a tent full of people.

*

I hadn't driven the Renault since repairing the wheel and I was apprehensive about its mechanical condition. After I started the engine, it began to heat up, but flushing the radiator a few times cured the problem.

Early on the day of our journey to Bergamo, Mr Marino told us we were always welcome to stay at their home and begged us to come back after the festival. I thanked him and said if we found no other immediate work, we'd be grateful to come back.

After waving our goodbyes as we drove out of the gateway to the house, it felt good to be back on the road again. The mechanical state of the Renault worried me a bit and I drove with extra care, listening for any abnormal noises coming from the rear. But the wheels stayed on and the engine didn't overheat. We arrived at the circus ground in Bergamo two hours later. Although we'd only done galas, stage and TV work during the last couple of years, I felt immediately comfortable in the familiar surroundings and circus atmosphere.

At first, when we started rehearsals, I was a little afraid the jump from the street to a circus ring would be a problem for Altan, but it didn't seem to affect him in the least and only helped to substantiate my view that he was already a professional. One joyous detail I had forgotten was the added lift the music brought to the work. Also, I was glad to have Pascale back in the act.

To my surprise, on opening night I didn't experience stage fright. In its place was a kind of positive, nervous energy, eager to show off our new way of portraying the act. With that energy radiating out, touching the audience, complemented by Altan's charm, Tacki's cheekiness and Pascale's impeccable portrayal as the classy French lady, we were a tremendous success – greater than we had ever been before.

One of the things Altan had done in the street was to saunter over to the people standing around, wagging his tail and sniffing them one by one. He did the same thing that evening, stretching his nose over the front boxes that circled the ring. The public loved this touch of affection from him, and they gave theirs in return.

During the second week of the festival, we received a phone call from Jocelyn, the secretary of the Tavel agency in Paris.

"We heard how well your new dog is working. Would you like to do a TV show in Santiago de Chile?"

"Chile! My God, that's the other side of the world – er, yes, of course," I interjected quickly.

"Okay then, that's good. You will fly Air France from Paris Charles de Gaulle. It's a sixteen-hour flight, but don't worry, Johnny Martin who worked in the Lido flew to Santiago for a TV show and said it was perfectly safe for his dogs." That news was reassuring because Johnny Martin had a famous vaudeville dog act and was someone who I knew cared a great deal for his animals.

Pascale was enthusiastic about the work. From then on she threw herself wholeheartedly into doing everything she could to help us continue and make the act better. I felt that all of a sudden, we were on a roll – even though a mere month before we'd had practically no act, and just two weeks before that we were working in the street, passing round the hat. Now, here we were with the prospect of jet-setting to another continent and being put up in a first-class hotel to perform in a TV show. The round trip would take one week and we would earn more money than if we had worked in the street for six months.

With no immediate engagement following the circus festival, we went back to Antonio's parents' place. It was the beginning of September. In ten days we would leave for the Chile job. We could have gone back to working in the street, but for all the good it had been for us, I wanted to put that phase of our lives behind us. It was something necessary at the time and pertinent to evolving the act, but that is how I wanted to keep it – I didn't want it to become a way of life for us.

I spent those few days left at Antonio's place making the props look good and arranging for the other dogs to be looked after while we were away. We decided to leave our cat, Hansi, in the trailer, leaving a window slightly ajar for him to come and go as he pleased. Antonio agreed to feed him. I was confident Hansi wouldn't run away.

The money we'd earned at the festival was enough to see us through until the TV show, so it was also a time for us to relax a little and enjoy our newfound financial security. During that time, two more offers of work came from agencies who either heard how good the act was or had actually seen us working in Bergamo. Things were finally really moving again.

*

And so it was. Six months after doing the Morocco job, we found ourselves at Charles de Gaulle airport waiting for our flight to Santiago. The red tape of getting the props through customs and seeing Altan and Tacki safely into their flight kennels made us nervous, reminiscent of our last time with the dogs in an airport. I was afraid Pascale would start to cry again. I looked at her and smiled. Pascale, seeing the irony of the situation, smiled back. With a new feeling of confidence, we crossed through passport control.

I settled into my seat and pondered the events that had transpired since we last sat in an aircraft six months ago. Keeping the loving memory of Bush locked in my thoughts, I thought of Altan, my hero, down in the hold, knowing we had found a new star for the act. We were on our way – not only to do the TV show in Chile, but, thanks to the street, to a new, better way of working.

*

And here I am, a few months later…

Darkness comes early to Scandinavia in October, and the cold wind blowing across the car park begins to bite my ears. Immersed in all my memories, I've lost track of the time. The last rays of sunshine have long since gone, replaced now by the luminosity of the street lighting.

I must get back. Pascale will be waiting to go out for an evening meal and the dogs need to be fed and taken for a walk. Tomorrow we will make our way back to Normandy. Altan is a real pro, and the TV show in Chile was a tremendous success. Work is flowing in our direction again. To be prepared for the future, we've acquired a bearded collie named Theo and rescued a mixed fox terrier to train for the act; we named him Billy. In one week we will take another plane trip, only this time it will be with all the dogs and most of our belongings: our diversion from circus to other forms of entertainment has come full circle. I have just signed a contract with the Big Apple Circus to perform at Lincoln Center.

New York City!

It's an offer we can't refuse. And that will be followed by a two-year contract with Ringling Bros, Barnum & Bailey Circus – The Greatest Show on Earth – the same show in which Dad had been booked before his untimely death. So that has also come full circle, and I will be carrying on where Dad left off.

We have mixed feelings about leaving Europe, as well as apprehension about a different way of life in America. On the other hand, we are feeling great excitement at the thought of working in front of American audiences.

We will have to leave Barny behind, but that can't be helped for the moment. He has reached the ripe old age of twenty-eight, and I don't want to risk subjecting him to the rigors of quarantine.

I look about me a last time at the car park and try to visualise the proud old circus building again. It has been many years since I felt this close to Dad's act and I'm reluctant to leave, to end my pilgrimage. In one last effort to touch them, to be close to them, I imagine their phantom outlines on the bare tarmac: Dad playing

Old Regnas with aplomb and studied clumsiness; Prince knocking down the wooden boxes; Candy winding her way in between Dad's legs; the first Barny pulling the cart. What a wonderful legacy my father left me and my adventurous little troupe.

The vivid memories and nostalgia that engulfed me a while ago have finally faded, and now all I can see is the black tarmac with the white lines. I shiver, but I linger a bit longer until finally all the memories are exhausted and my need to revisit the past, satisfied. Then I get up and start back towards the hotel.